I0015301

Robo-Advisor with Python

A hands-on guide to building and operating your own
Robo-advisor

Aki Ranin

BIRMINGHAM—MUMBAI

Robo-Advisor with Python

Copyright © 2023 Packt Publishing

Group Product Manager: Reshma Raman

Publishing Product Manager: Apeksha Shetty

Content Development Editor: Manikandan Kurup

Technical Editor: Sweety Pagaria

Copy Editor: Safis Editing

Project Coordinator: Farheen Fathima

Proofreader: Safis Editing

Indexer: Rekha Nair

Production Designer: Shankar Kalbhor

Marketing Coordinator: Nivedita Singh

First published: February 2023

Production reference: 1230223

Published by Packt Publishing Ltd.
Livery Place
35 Livery Street
Birmingham
B3 2PB, UK.

ISBN 978-1-80181-969-5

www.packtpub.com

Contributors

About the author

Aki Ranin is the founder of two AI start-ups in Singapore: Bambu in fintech and Healthzilla in healthtech. He serves as an adjunct lecturer on the topic of machine learning at Singapore Management University. His company Bambu has been a pioneer of Robo-advisor platforms since 2016, having built the first Robo-advisor in Singapore and worked with over 20 enterprise clients across the world to design, build, and launch Robo-advisors.

Aki lives in Singapore, holds a master's degree in computer science from Aalto University in Finland, and occasionally writes about start-ups, philosophy, and technology.

About the reviewers

Pierre Valentin CFA is the chief product officer at Bambu, a Singapore-based Robo-advisory tech company. Previously, Pierre worked in wealth management for clients of all sizes, from priority banking to family offices. He is a strong advocate of passive investments and diversification.

Jason Jisu Park CFA is a director at the Chief Investment Office (CIO) of Bank of America. As a senior quantitative analyst, he constructs portfolios for the Merrill Edge Robo-advisory platform and the Merrill-managed Personal Retirement Strategy 401(k) accounts. He received an M.S. in Financial Engineering from Columbia University and a B.S. in Industrial and Systems Engineering with the highest honor from Georgia Institute of Technology.

Table of Contents

3

Robo-Advisor Platforms versus Algorithms   27

4

Leasing, Buying, or Building Your Own Robo-Advisor   35

Part 2: Building Your Own Robo-Advisor

5

Basic Setup and Requirements for Building a Robo-Advisor   47

6

Goal-Based Investing 57

7

Risk Profiling and Scoring 75

8

Model Portfolio Construction 89

9

Investment Projections 113

Part 3: Running and Operating Your Own Robo-Advisor

13

14

15

16

Preface

Robo-advisors are becoming table stakes for the wealth management industry across all segments, from retail to high-net-worth investors. This is because they enable you to manage your own portfolio and financial institution to create automated platforms for effective digital portfolio management. This book is your hands-on guide to understanding how robo-advisors work, and how to build one efficiently. The chapters are designed in a way to help you get a comprehensive grasp of what robo-advisors do and how they are structured with an end-to-end workflow.

You'll begin by learning about the key decisions that influence the building of a robo-advisor, along with considerations on building versus licensing a platform. As you advance, you'll find out how to build all the core capabilities of a robo-advisor using Python, including goals, risk questionnaires, portfolios, and projections. The book also shows you how to create orders, as well as open accounts and perform KYC verification for transacting. Finally, you'll be able to implement capabilities such as performance reporting and rebalancing for operating a robo-advisor with ease.

By the end of this book, you'll have gained a solid understanding of how robo-advisors work and be well on your way to building one for yourself or your business.

Who this book is for

This book is for finance professionals with a basic knowledge of Python, developers who are interested in building their own Robo-advisor to manage personal investments or build a platform for their business to operate, and product managers and business leaders within businesses who are looking to lease, buy, or build a Robo-advisor.

> **Disclaimer**
>
> It is important to remind you that this book is not investment advice, nor is any such advice intended in any of its content. If you choose to make investments on the basis of this book, it is your responsibility alone. Similarly, if you choose to use any contents of this book, you alone will be responsible for any bugs, quality issues, investment outcomes, and/or regulatory compliance.

What this book covers

Chapter 1, *Introduction to Robo-Advisors*, will help you understand what a Robo-advisor is, why it exists, and how it works. We will cover the history of Robo-advisors to educate you on how these platforms have become popular, and why they have become an essential part of wealth management today.

Chapter 2, *What Makes Up a Robo-Advisor?*, will serve as a broad introduction to the inner workings of a Robo-advisor, and how the different parts relate to each other. This will serve as a reference during *Part 2*, when we build out each of these components.

Chapter 3, *Robo-Advisor Platforms versus Algorithms*, will help different types of readers understand how the core algorithms underlying a Robo-advisor are necessary but not sufficient to build a commercial Robo-advisor platform.

Chapter 4, *Leasing, Buying, or Building Your Own Robo-Advisor*, will help you decide whether you should be building your own Robo-advisor or using commercially available platforms.

Chapter 5, *Basic Setup and Requirements to Build a Robo-Advisor*, will establish the tools, skills, and technologies needed to complete the hands-on part of the book.

Chapter 6, *Goal-Based Investing*, will introduce the key concept of goals, as it relates to investing. We will look at how we can model different types of goals as investments, to use later on in transacting.

Chapter 7, *Risk Profiling and Scoring*, will look at ways to quantify risk for investments and how to score the risk appetite for investors.

Chapter 8, *Model Portfolio Construction*, will teach you how to create portfolios from individual investment products such as **exchange-traded funds** (**ETFs**) , and how to use portfolios with risk scoring in your Robo-advisor.

Chapter 9, *Investment Projections*, will teach you how to calculate and visualize projections for investments using your model portfolios. We will show possible outcomes given certain investment time horizons and amounts.

Chapter 10, *Account Opening and KYC*, will teach you how to open accounts and perform **Know Your Customer** (**KYC**) verification with brokers for the purposes of transacting your portfolios.

Chapter 11, *Funding Your Account*, will teach you about different ways in which you can fund your investment account.

Chapter 12, *Order Management and Execution*, will teach you how to create, manage, and execute orders for your portfolios.

Chapter 13, *Performance Reporting*, will show you how Robo-advisors are not manual algorithms but are automated to ensure the portfolio is consistently in good standing. This chapter covers the additional requirements to run and operate a Robo-advisor continuously.

Chapter 14, Rebalancing, will teach you about one of the core capabilities of any Robo-advisor: rebalancing. This ensures the portfolio stays close to the original model portfolio, despite market fluctuations between asset classes.

Chapter 15, Dividends and Fee Management, will show you that, in addition to orders and rebalancing, we should take care to calculate dividends from the underlying products in our portfolio, and charge appropriate fees where necessary.

Chapter 16, Regulations for Robo-Advisors, will wrap it all up, and explore the regulatory requirements to operate various types of Robo-advisors.

To get the most out of this book

You will need a basic understanding of investment principles and of Python development.

Software/hardware covered in the book	Operating system requirements
Google Colab	Windows, macOS, or Linux
Python	Google Chrome (preferred)

If you are using the digital version of this book, we advise you to type the code yourself or access the code from the book's GitHub repository (a link is available in the next section). Doing so will help you avoid any potential errors related to the copying and pasting of code.

Download the example code files

You can download the example code files for this book from GitHub at `https://github.com/PacktPublishing/Robo-Advisor-with-Python`. If there's an update to the code, it will be updated in the GitHub repository.

We also have other code bundles from our rich catalog of books and videos available at `https://github.com/PacktPublishing/`. Check them out!

Conventions used

There are a number of text conventions used throughout this book.

`Code in text`: Indicates code words in text, database table names, folder names, filenames, file extensions, pathnames, dummy URLs, user input, and Twitter handles. Here is an example: "Let's install another module called `mplfinance`."

A block of code is set as follows:

```
stocks = Allocation("SPY", 0.6)
bonds = Allocation("TLT", 0.4)
myPortfolio = Portfolio("Growth", 4)
myPortfolio.allocations.append(stocks)
myPortfolio.allocations.append(bonds)
df = myPortfolio.getDailyPrices("20y")
```

When we wish to draw your attention to a particular part of a code block, the relevant lines or items are set in bold:

```
for index, value in sectorLabels.iteritems():
    sectorLabels[index]=(value.capitalize().replace("_"," "))
plt.pie(sectorWeights, labels = sectorLabels)
plt.show()
```

Bold: Indicates a new term, an important word, or words that you see onscreen. For instance, words in menus or dialog boxes appear in **bold**. Here is an example: "In fact, Colab will then automatically create a **Colab Notebooks** folder under **My Drive**, which will store all your Colab files going forward."

> **Tips or important notes**
> Appear like this.

Get in touch

Feedback from our readers is always welcome.

General feedback: If you have questions about any aspect of this book, email us at customercare@packtpub.com and mention the book title in the subject of your message.

Errata: Although we have taken every care to ensure the accuracy of our content, mistakes do happen. If you have found a mistake in this book, we would be grateful if you would report this to us. Please visit www.packtpub.com/support/errata and fill in the form.

Piracy: If you come across any illegal copies of our works in any form on the internet, we would be grateful if you would provide us with the location address or website name. Please contact us at copyright@packt.com with a link to the material.

If you are interested in becoming an author: If there is a topic that you have expertise in and you are interested in either writing or contributing to a book, please visit authors.packtpub.com.

Share Your Thoughts

Once you've read *Robo-Advisor with Python*, we'd love to hear your thoughts! Scan the QR code below to go straight to the Amazon review page for this book and share your feedback.

https://packt.link/r/1-801-81969-6

Your review is important to us and the tech community and will help us make sure we're delivering excellent quality content.

Download a free PDF copy of this book

Thanks for purchasing this book!

Do you like to read on the go but are unable to carry your print books everywhere? Is your eBook purchase not compatible with the device of your choice?

Don't worry, now with every Packt book you get a DRM-free PDF version of that book at no cost.

Read anywhere, any place, on any device. Search, copy, and paste code from your favorite technical books directly into your application.

The perks don't stop there, you can get exclusive access to discounts, newsletters, and great free content in your inbox daily

Follow these simple steps to get the benefits:

1. Scan the QR code or visit the link below

https://packt.link/free-ebook/978-1-80181-969-5

2. Submit your proof of purchase
3. That's it! We'll send your free PDF and other benefits to your email directly

Part 1: The Basic Elements of Robo-Advisors

The first part of the book will lay the groundwork by explaining the purpose, context, and key concepts of Robo-advisors.

This section has the following chapters:

- *Chapter 1, Introduction to Robo-Advisors*
- *Chapter 2, What Makes Up a Robo-Advisor?*
- *Chapter 3, Robo-Advisor Platforms versus Algorithms*
- *Chapter 4, Leasing, Buying, or Building Your Own Robo-Advisor*

Introduction to Robo-Advisors

Welcome to the world of Robo-advisors. My name is **Aki Ranin**, and I'll be your guide on this journey into digital investing. I started a Robo-advisor company called Bambu in 2016, and have been working on Robo-advisor solutions ever since. I hope my experiences will be of use to you on your digital wealth journey.

In this very first chapter, I'll provide an overview of Robo-advisors. We will then understand why they were created, and why people use them. By the end of this chapter, you'll have a good understanding of why Robo-advisors exist.

Throughout this book, we'll proceed to tackle the main questions you might have while embarking on your own Robo-advisor project, from the overall strategy to the key capabilities demonstrated in Python.

In this chapter, we're going to cover the following topics:

- What is a Robo-advisor?
- How do Robo-advisors work?
- What is the history of Robo-advisors?
- Why are Robo-advisors an essential part of the wealth management industry?

What is a Robo-advisor?

Today, Robo-advisors take many shapes and forms, but fundamentally, we are talking about a digital investment platform. An individual investor, such as yourself, uses a Robo-advisor to manage investments on your behalf. While there is no formal or legal definition for a Robo-advisor, a typical Robo-advisor will help you make investment decisions using a digital app or website. To make investments, you will be required to transfer real money into an account managed by the Robo-advisor. Consequently, that money will be placed into some form of investment product, most often into an investment portfolio of **Exchange Traded Funds (ETFs)**. While in certain scenarios it may be possible to use other products, such as stocks or mutual funds, ETFs are the main products powering Robo-advisors due to their low cost, diversification, high liquidity, and daily price transparency.

Such a seemingly simple tool is helpful to investors for several reasons:

- **Access**: Traditionally, to make investments, you would have to have a physical interaction of some sort with a financial institution. Initially, this would be done by walking into a branch office, but later by getting in touch with such an institution over the phone or via email. Either way, the inconvenience of these interactions is greatly improved by digital tools such as apps or websites. Further, this access was traditionally limited to the wealthy. To justify a human financial advisor spending time on a customer to manage their investments, significant fees had to be incurred by the customer. This is equally true today, and due to inflation, the time of a professional investment manager has never been more expensive. Further, this cost, which was a percentage of assets, meant that to open an account, you had to start with large sums of investible cash – up to 7 figures for premiere advisors from private banks. Most Robo-advisors have minimum account sizes of just a few hundred dollars, making them accessible to regular people without huge existing savings. In between, some banks and wealth managers may offer so-called hybrid advice, which combines digital platforms with limited human management.

- **Convenience**: While anyone could learn to invest on their own, most people choose not to. If you're a busy professional, or simply have better ways to spend your time than reading annual reports like Warren Buffett, then you don't have the time to not only research the market but learn the tools of the trade used by professional investors. Apps such as Robinhood have made it easy to make investments, but at the end of the day, are you comfortable making those decisions on your own? If you stick with index funds, then which ones do you buy, and in which ratios? Even simple investing involves a huge amount of decision-making. Robo-advisors simplify the process of investing by abstracting away things such as portfolio and order management and instead ask you about how you feel about risk. The rest is taken care of on your behalf.

- **Cost**: Robo-advisors typically charge a small percentage of your total assets on the platform as an annual fee. Compared to traditional investment advisors, who might charge as high as a few percent per year at the high end, or typically around 1%, a Robo-advisor might charge you a fraction of a percent. This is, again, largely driven by automation – there is simply less human cost required to manage your account. On paper, if you already know what you're doing, you could save even more by building a portfolio of ETFs on a low-cost online broker. It just means you will have to also invest the time to track performance and perform rebalancing, and that time is money too. To further justify their fees, many Robo-advisors offer additional conveniences such as tax reporting and optimization.

- **Psychology**: If you've never invested before, you may not yet be familiar with this problem. This has been an area of research for decades, and there are many known traps that investors fall into when they manage their investments. These include the sunk cost fallacy and the loss aversion bias. Humans aren't all the same, but all of us have our own set of biases and quirks that make it very challenging to remain objective when it comes to making decisions about money. The benefit of a Robo-advisor in this regard is that it simply removes a lot of this decision-making from you, instead relying on compound interest, some simple math, and time to produce a return on your investment.

These are just the fundamental principles behind the design of the first generation of Robo-advisors. Many of these platforms now also offer other services and products, such as debit cards, loans, and the ability to trade single stocks and crypto. Over time, your financial life may increasingly revolve around your Robo-advisor.

Now that we have an idea of why Robo-advisors were created, we should look into how they work, and the various components that are required to build one.

How does a Robo-advisor work?

Our ultimate goal is to build a Robo-advisor, so we must begin to unpack the concept into its constituent parts. We will dedicate lots more time to this question in *Chapter 2, What Makes Up a Robo-Advisor?*, and beyond, but to set the stage, let's establish some basics. The core features of any Robo-advisor include:

- An app or website user interface
- Questionnaires for profile information, risk appetite, and **Know Your Customer** (**KYC**)
- Portfolio modeling, construction, and recommendation
- Automated account opening, management, and transfers
- Automated order management, execution, and rebalancing
- Performance modeling and monitoring
- Reporting and statements

Fundamentally, what makes a Robo-advisor a Robo-advisor is the element of automation. It's not simply making investing digital, as that has been done before and is being done today. If there are just humans on both sides of the screen making all the decisions, then it's not considered a Robo-advisor. Mind you, you can have something called a **hybrid Robo-advisor**, which is just to indicate that there are different degrees to which this automation can be done. Initially, the plan was for Robo-advisors to be fully automated. Effectively, the customer using the Robo-advisor would be interacting with nothing but technology and algorithms making investment decisions. The later addition of **hybrid** implies a higher degree of human involvement in the form of a financial advisor. Both flavors of Robo-advisors continue to exist and thrive today.

The core investment decision being made is what to invest in. Such questions are traditionally highly regulated by government entities whose exact roles and guidance vary by country. This guidance has been clarified over the past decade as it relates to how Robo-advisors are allowed to operate in their decision-making. For example, you might imagine that some fancy artificial intelligence is making the investment decisions inside of a Robo-advisor. I used to get that question a lot, myself. The regulations tend to forbid that explicitly in favor of clear rules on how investment decisions must be made based on risk scoring. The most common form of risk scoring is a simple questionnaire. Depending on how a customer answers this questionnaire, they will be placed into conservative, moderate, or aggressive investments. These terms simply indicate the amount of risk a customer is willing to accept when making investments and is then the basis for the Robo-advisor allocating customers to specific investments matching that risk score.

We'll get into all of that in much more detail later when we get hands-on, but before that, let's go back to the beginning to understand how this all started.

Origins of the Robo-advisor

The term Robo-advisor has become quite ubiquitous in the past decade since digital investing has become mainstream. During the COVID-19 pandemic in particular, amid market turmoil, the popularity of investing reached new highs. While most of this newfound attention was directed toward trading tech stocks on platforms such as Robinhood in America, it was also a record period of growth for many Robo-advisors. During the peak frenzy, Robinhood reached a record one million downloads in a single day (Haverstock and Konrad). Robo-advisors may have not yet reached such levels of excitement among retail investors, yet after more than a decade of steady growth globally, Robo-advisors are here to stay.

The term Robo-advisor is both helpful and misleading. There are no robots involved, even if automation of the financial advisor is implied. The exact origin is not known, but the earliest reference comes from a financial journal article in 2001 (Kane). The first platforms we would call by the term only emerged in 2010, in the wake of the financial crisis and riding a new wave of excitement for financial technology (Stein). In many ways, the Robo–advisor was inevitable. Like any other industry, the wealth management industry was due for digital transformation. Any process mainly driven by humans and paper is bound to be disrupted by digital platforms looking to optimize time and cost.

Now, let's review the path Robo-advisors have taken from the early days, and where they seem to be heading today.

Evolution of the Robo-advisor

The first two Robo-advisors were **Betterment** and **Wealthfront**. They both started in 2010, and for at least 5 years, they were the main two actors responsible for starting a new industry. Their marketing was consistently aimed at the next generation of would-be investors: the millennials. Among the incumbents, this was seen as the wrong strategy. Millennials simply did not have the assets, which were largely held by their parents and grandparents. Nevertheless, the users and assets of both platforms kept climbing year after year.

Eventually, many of the incumbents, such as **Schwab** and **Blackrock**, entered the market with Robo-advisors and have since overtaken these pioneers in sheer **Assets Under Management** (**AUM**). Yet the role of these two start-ups cannot be overstated. Many Robo-advisors operating today have copied their approach, marketing, portfolios, and user experience directly from these two platforms. At the beginning of 2022, UBS announced it had acquired Wealthfront for $1.4 billion to focus on millennials and the Gen Z that came after them (UBS). However, this acquisition was later terminated in September 2022 due to pressure from regulators and shareholders (Reuters).

Let's briefly wind back the clock and examine how we've arrived in a situation where Robo-advisors are being adopted worldwide and becoming integrated into the suite of basic financial products available to most consumers alongside credit and savings.

From consumer platforms to B2B

My journey with Robo-advisors started in 2015 in Singapore, where I was working as a software consultant at the time. Many of my clients were financial institutions, and there was a tangible hype building around this idea of Robo-advisors. The question on everyone's mind was, would Silicon Valley startups come across the oceans to challenge the traditional distribution networks operated by the major banks across Asia, or would local competition emerge? The term used for this type of phenomenon is *disruption*, and the people in charge don't like it. This forced the existing players to evaluate whether they should be building platforms and pre-empt any new entrants from stealing market share.

From this hype, it gradually became clear that Robo-advisors were not a separate category of financial service. They represented the digital transformation of the industry, which was still largely operating in the world before the internet. Major banks only offered wealth management services through advisors to affluent or high-net-worth clients. At best, retail clients were offered high-priced online brokerage services with terrible user experiences. This combination of factors created the need for Robo-advisor platforms, such as my company Bambu. Some of the world's largest banks might have the appetite and budget to dedicate a team for 5 to 10 years and build their own Robo-advisor from scratch, but what about the rest? Since 2016, companies such as Bambu, InvestCloud, and WeInvest have been offering technologies and services to financial institutions looking to launch Robo-advisors around the world.

From America to the rest of the world

If the first Robo-advisors were launched as early as 2010 in America, why did it take so many years for them to spread to the rest of the world? If anything, the choices for retail investors outside of America are far more limited. Even if you know what you're doing, many countries do not have low-cost online brokers that offer access to low-cost ETFs to build a portfolio. When I lived in Singapore, in 2016, my bank would charge me $15 for every trade, which isn't uncommon in many places even today. This goes a long way to explain the popularity of apps such as Robinhood that offer *free* trading.

So, why doesn't every country have a Robo-advisor or several? Why haven't Betterment and Wealthfront conquered the world as Uber and PayPal have? The simple answer is *regulation*. Compared to taxis and payments, which are also regulated industries, wealth management is highly regulated. Not only that, but the regulations vary greatly between countries. What is allowed in America is not automatically allowed anywhere else. A Robo-advisor wishing to enter a new market must start by applying for local licensing, and ensuring their platform and business comply with local regulations. This process not only takes a huge amount of time and money but takes away focus from your immediate growth plans. Thus, for most platforms, until the growth opportunity is fully sapped locally, going international just isn't worth the trouble.

This introduces a massive hurdle for market entry, which plays into the hands of the incumbents and local startups. The pace of innovation for Robo-advisors thus far has been dictated by local start-up disruption. As soon as local Robo-advisors start emerging and gaining traction, the traditional providers must move to offer similar platforms and services. In Singapore, this process was driven largely by StashAway, which also started in 2016 as a start-up Robo-advisor. Initially, they were met with skepticism, but after a few years of solid growth, they have forced the hand of the industry and created a thriving ecosystem of Robo-advisors offered by a host of banks and start-ups playing catchup with StashAway.

From risk to goal-based investing

Traditionally, financial advisors would make a large part of their fees from commissions by selling specific fund products from asset managers. Hence, the engagement with new clients would center around which funds would be appropriate given the client's needs. In the early 2000s, academics started developing an investment methodology that catered more to the client's life situation than the advisor's incentives. One such methodology is **goal-based investing**. According to author Paolo Sironi, goal-based investing had never caught on due to two main reasons: the practice of selling investment products was still immensely successful, and the technology to create a compelling user experience wasn't there (Sironi). Robo-advisors presented a solution to the latter challenge.

Over the last decade, some form of goal-based investing has become the default approach for Robo-advisors around the world. Back in 2016, when Bambu was starting out, this was not an obvious choice. Many financial institutions were still operating in the traditional fund sales regime, so moving to goal-based investing was an additional unknown. Adding goals to a digital wealth platform is a double-edged sword. The obvious benefit is that it allows the platform to engage with the user around an aspirational topic of what they wish to achieve in their life, whereas the traditional engagement around risk is perceived as somewhat negative. The downside of adding goals to a user journey is that it is an additional complication. You still need risk questions, so the overall number of steps to open an account is now longer, which can impact conversion negatively.

The implementations of goal-based investing vary greatly among Robo-advisors. It can be as simple as assigning a name to your portfolio, or as complicated as assigning separate accounts and risk profiles to each goal. At Bambu, we made this the central defining feature of our platform, creating a whole library of calculator APIs to help people understand how much they might need for common life goals such as weddings, college, buying a home, or retiring based on different levels of lifestyle.

The future of Robo-advisors

Looking at where we are in 2022, a few key trends have emerged among the innovators in Robo-advisory. As market conditions and interest rates continue their turbulence, Robo-advisors are looking to expand their product offerings. A few years ago, this started with high-yield savings when Goldman Sachs entered the game with their Marcus app, offering 2% interest on cash. The success of this model forced many existing Robo-advisors to offer similar savings plans, and it was one of the reasons for record growth in users and AUM between 2019 and 2020. The savings rates offered by Wealthfront and others are highly dependent on interest rates and subject to regular updates (Wealthfront).

The fiscal pressures to deliver higher revenues and margins continue to push Robo-advisors to innovate and expand beyond their initial remit of investing. Several platforms have introduced bundles that include debit cards, margin loans, and even trading in stocks and crypto. These additional features serve to keep clients engaged, boost margins, and increase overall wallet share. This product expansion is beginning to gray the traditional borders between financial institutions such as advisors, brokers, custodians, lenders, and banks. Increasingly, these players are entering each other's segments with overlapping product offerings.

Longer term, we may also see a bigger transformation of the Robo-advisor through blockchain technology. While regulations do not yet allow allocations of cryptocurrencies as part of Robo-advisor portfolios, that may be around the corner soon. Betterment's acquisition of the crypto platform Makara indicates such a future (Sharma). However, the bigger opportunity may lie in a fundamental rethinking of how investment products are structured. The fundamental challenges in giving the world easy and free access to investing are still unsolved, due to the many complexities in how the industry operates, and the archaic technologies it was built on. Ideas such as tokenization promise a new approach to using distributed ledgers as a mechanism for defining the next generation of investment products. Already, many emerging markets have attracted stablecoin-based wallets as a solution to rampant inflation. Instead of the famous S&P 500 index fund, your future Robo-advisor might offer you portfolios consisting of tokens of fractional ownership in NFTs.

Summary

In this first chapter, we established the proper context for understanding what Robo-advisors are, where they came from, how they are useful, and how they have evolved since their beginnings in 2010. This should give you a basic understanding to follow the rest of the chapters in this book.

From here, we will delve deeper into the inner workings of the Robo-advisor before going hands-on and building one.

Further reading

You might be interested in reading some extra information related to the topics discussed in this chapter. Here are a few links to some of the external resources:

- Haverstock, Eliza, and Alex Konrad. *Robinhood Upping Emergency Funding To $3 Billion As Downloads Hit Record 1 Million Per Day.* Forbes, 1 February 2021: `https://www.forbes.com/sites/elizahaverstock/2021/02/01/exclusive-robinhood-secures-another-1-billion-in-funds-and-is-in-talks-for-more-as-downloads-hit-record-1-million-per-day/`.

- Kane, Libby. *Where the Term Robo-Advisor Started.* Business Insider, 5 September 2014: `https://www.businessinsider.com/where-robo-advisor-started-2014-9`.

- Sharma, Rakesh. *Digital Advisory Firm Betterment Enters Crypto With Makara Acquisition.* Investopedia, 11 February 2022: `https://www.investopedia.com/betterment-enters-crypto-with-makara-acquisition-5218550`.

- Sironi, Paolo. FinTech Innovation: From Robo-Advisors to Goal Based Investing and Gamification. Wiley, 2016: `https://www.wiley.com/en-us/FinTech+Innovation:+From+Robo+Advisors+to+Goal+Based+Investing+and+Gamification-p-9781119226987`.

- Stein, Jon. *The History of Betterment: Changing an Industry.* Betterment, 20 July 2016: `https://www.betterment.com/resources/the-history-of-betterment`.

- UBS. *UBS agrees to acquire Wealthfront to deliver digital wealth management offering to millennial and Gen Z affluent investors.* UBS, 26 January 2022: `https://www.ubs.com/global/en/media/display-page-ndp/en-20220126-wealthfront.html`.

- Reuters. *Shareholder, regulator pushback ended UBS-Wealthfront deal, SonntagsZeitung reports.* Reuters, 2 October 2022: `https://www.reuters.com/markets/deals/shareholder-regulator-pushback-ended-ubs-wealthfront-deal-paper-2022-10-02/`.

- Wealthfront. *The Wealthfront Cash Account Now Has a 3.80% APY.* Wealthfront Blog, 16 December 2022: `https://www.wealthfront.com/blog/cash-account-apy/`.

What Makes Up
a Robo-Advisor?

This is a key chapter, as we will define all the basic concepts and terminology needed to build a Robo-advisor. As you delve into specific implementation details in later chapters, this will be worth bookmarking as a general reference.

In this chapter, we will begin with learning about the elements that make up a Robo-advisor and how they fit together in a workflow. We will understand the impact of Goal-based investing on building a Robo-advisor. Going further, we will go through the basic concepts and purpose of risk profiling, portfolios, and projections, account opening, funding, order management, and execution. Finally, we will go through some basic concepts that are required to operate a Robo-advisor.

We will cover the following main topics in this chapter:

- Understanding the workflow of a standard Robo-advisor
- Introducing financial planning and Goal-based investing
- Defining risk profiling, portfolios, and projections
- Account opening, performing KYC and **Anti Money Laundering** (**AML**), and funding accounts
- Introducing order management and execution

Understanding the workflow of a standard Robo-advisor

To further our understanding of what functionality makes up a Robo-advisor, we will break up the various processes into individual steps. These are called workflows, and they represent a high-level view of how a system operates and is used by people.

The capabilities required for any Robo-advisor are dictated by two main sources – regulations set by government agencies and the practical requirements of a digital user experience. While it is the former that sets the more black-and-white requirements, it is typically the latter that defines how the various capabilities form a cohesive platform. Regulations mainly concern the types of information that is exchanged between a Robo-advisor and an investor. This introduces a natural dependency and order that dictates how we must build up a workflow for our Robo-advisor.

For the sake of simplicity, we will choose a singular workflow as the basis for the rest of our book. Every Robo-advisor will likely deviate from this precise ordering, due to local regulations or some differentiating capabilities created to separate themselves from the competition. Our workflow is going to be based on Goal-based investing, for reasons we will elaborate on shortly. In the following figure, you find a visual representation of the workflow we will be using.

Standard Robo-Advisor Workflow

Figure 2.1 – A standard Robo-advisor workflow

The following sections will cover each step, and from there, we will proceed to implement these sets of capabilities in later chapters. Now, let's begin with the first step of the process of financial planning.

Introducing financial planning and Goal-based investing

This marks the beginning and first touchpoint for our Robo-advisor. In this section, we'll cover the few questions investors might be greeted with upon opening our Robo-advisor.

As we established in the first chapter, Robo-advisors have evolved from purely risk-based financial planning to include the concept of Goals in Goal-based investing. The latter is purely optional; you can certainly build and run a Robo-advisor without any Goals. Today, most Robo-advisors have adopted Goals because it helps their customers, the investors, structure an investment plan that relates to their own ambitions in life.

Therefore, the most basic version of financial planning on a Robo-advisor is to simply ask how much money you would like to invest. Regulations may differ on the minimum information required to justify an investment, but the following numbers will be required for later steps in the workflow:

- **Initial Investment**: How much cash are you willing to risk upfront?
- **Regular Savings Plan (RSP)**: How much cash are you willing to add each month?
- **Target Date**: When will you need the investment money to be withdrawn?
- **Target Amount**: What is the investment amount you are aiming to accumulate?

> **Note**
> Strictly speaking, monthly savings are not mandatory for a Robo-advisor, but most platforms do support this, as many users might not have significant cash available to invest right now. Therefore, it makes sense to save some cash monthly to increase your investment over time.

When you do add Goals to a Robo-advisor, there are a few things to consider. If you wanted to keep things as simple as possible, then you could just add a name to your investment. For example, you might ask the investor what the investment is for. The investor might decide to invest $10,000 for retirement. That's perfectly fine.

Fundamentally, the role of financial planning, whether performed by a Robo-advisor or a human financial advisor, is to assist the investor in answering the *what* and *how* questions about their futures. Goals represent answers to what an investor might choose to do with their money in the future. The trickier question of the two is how that might be possible financially.

For example, a $10,000 investment for retirement is a fantastic start if you're 25 years old because you will have several decades of compound interest to grow that investment into something meaningful at retirement age. Conversely, the same investment at age 55 will not be a viable solution for growing a retirement nest egg by age 65; that's only 10 years of compound interest.

Questionnaires for Goals

It quickly becomes clear that if we are committed to financial planning, then we must understand more about how much money will be needed for the Goal, and when it will be needed. Once you go down the rabbit hole of modeling Goals, the list of questions around a retirement Goal will include the following:

- What age are you now?
- When do you plan to retire?
- How much will you need in retirement to pay for your cost of living?
- Will you take care of only yourself or a spouse or other dependents?
- How will taxes impact your retirement income?
- Do you have social security to assist with the retirement cost of living?
- How much are you able to invest now?
- How much are you able to invest on a monthly basis?

To further complicate matters, most investors will never have thought through these questions and may not have answers readily available. For example, the question of how much your monthly expenses might be in retirement depends on factors such as inflation and, ultimately, life expectancy. If we make some assumptions about these factors from reliable government sources, then we can reformulate the question of retirement expenses into a form that is easier to respond to, such as what your preferred retirement lifestyle is.

The end result of financial planning is that by asking the right questions and by making some assumptions, we can produce the numbers required to make any investment – initial investment, regular savings plan, target date, and target amount. By going through the preceding questionnaire, the investor may have come out with a much higher figure than they assumed, especially for an expensive, long-term Goal such as retirement.

Because retail investors with little to no experience will certainly need such assistance, my company Bambu has invested years of effort in building up such a capability, which we call **Goal helpers**. Effectively, each Goal helper provides a series of questions that will produce the same investment plan outputs of initial investment, a regular savings plan, a target date, and a target amount. The questions will be different for Goals such as retirement, college education, starting a business, taking a gap year, going on a dream holiday, buying a home, and getting married.

Goal-based investing will also impact several processes further in the workflow, which we will examine in the rest of this chapter, including risk profiling, projections, and account opening.

Defining risk profiling, portfolios, and projections

In this section, we'll learn about the basic building blocks of any investment – risk and portfolios.

You may be surprised to learn that despite all the innovation around how investing is done in 2022, the fundamental principles of how investments are made haven't changed since 1952. That is the date of Harry Markowitz's famous thesis paper simply titled *Portfolio Selection* (Markowitz). It outlines the principles used by nearly all investment advisors today, including Robo-advisors. The significance of this work eventually saw him awarded the 1990 Nobel Prize in Economics.

Modern portfolio theory

Before we dive into the specifics of Markowitz's theory, now named **Modern Portfolio Theory** (**MPT**), we should stop to ask ourselves why we need a portfolio to begin with. Can't we just invest in stocks like people on Robinhood? Well, technically speaking, any investment that contains more than one investment product is a portfolio, whether you treat it as such or not. If you took the advice of Warren Buffett and simply invested all your money into a single product, the S&P 500 index fund, it's still a portfolio. Why? Because like it says on the tin, that ETF is composed of the 500 largest publicly listed stocks in America. So, unless you literally put all your money into one asset, say Bitcoin, you simply can't get away from portfolios.

What did Harry Markowitz tell us about managing our portfolios? While it may seem somewhat obvious that, for any investment, you would want to maximize your investment returns while taking a minimal risk, the challenge is implementing that in practice. This is what MPT provides us, a practical framework for calculating risk that we can use to determine an optimal makeup for our portfolio. Markowitz makes a number of famous assumptions in his paper, the first of which is called **diversification**. It simply means that to find a balance between risk and reward, your portfolio should contain different types of investments – some high-risk and high-reward, and some low-risk and low-reward. To make this actionable, he chooses the metric of correlation to determine whether investments are different or not.

According to MPT, if we assume a portfolio of multiple potential investments, to find our optimal portfolio, we need three inputs:

- **Expected returns**: This is a simple weighted sum of the average annualized returns for each investment in the portfolio. It is a proxy for how much return we should expect in the future from these investments.

- **Variance**: Markowitz's choice of proxy for calculating risk is how much variance the returns of the investment have shown, which means whether they are stable or wildly fluctuating.

- **Correlation**: Using the preceding metrics of return and variance, we can calculate the covariance between investments in the portfolio, which indicates whether the investments are moving up or down in unison, in opposite directions, or randomly.

The end result of MPT is what's called an **efficient frontier**, which is a plotted graph that allows us to find the optimal mix of investment products in our portfolio to maximize our expected returns in relation to risk. We will do this all hands-on in *Chapter 8, Model Portfolio Construction*. For the time being, let's move on to the next steps in our Robo-advisor workflow.

Risk questionnaires

Before we can talk about which products to choose for our portfolios, and ultimately which portfolio to choose for our investor, we must elaborate further on risk. As we've just established variance as a metric for risk, we need to know how much variance is right for the investor.

Certainly, one approach is to simply ask the investor to choose from an available list of portfolios with varying degrees of return and risk. In fact, many Robo-advisors still do that. The one limitation is that, in most jurisdictions, such educated choices are typically limited to so-called accredited investors. This is a legal term that hints at some type of verification of expertise but is, in fact, a simple measure of wealth in most cases.

In most cases, for retail investors, a more elaborate approach is required by law. This might come in the form of a mandatory questionnaire, or a minimal set of questions required to quantify how much risk an investor is willing to accept. In other countries, it may be a set of guidelines around how such risk scoring should be done, often on the basis of factors such as risk tolerance, risk capacity, and risk score. Let's briefly define these terms:

- **Risk tolerance**: A direct quantifiable measure of how much financial risk an investor is willing to accept, typically calculated on the basis of a standardized questionnaire

- **Risk capacity**: An indirect quantifiable measure of how much financial risk an investor can take without becoming reckless, typically calculated from other metrics such as age, income, and previous investment experience

- **Risk score**: An often proprietary algorithm to combine outputs of risk tolerance and risk capacity, standardized to a range such as 1–5, 1–10, or 1–100.

Portfolio construction and allocation

Before we can allocate investors into portfolios, we must build our portfolios. As we learned from Markowitz, the basis of constructing any portfolio should be proper diversification. In practice, this typically means diversification along multiple dimensions of potential investment products, such as the following:

- **Asset class**: This is just a way to separate different types of investible assets, the classics being stocks, bonds, and commodities. You can get as granular as you like, of course. While regulations currently limit the inclusion of cryptocurrencies, that seems a likely addition to future portfolios sooner rather than later.

- **Asset region**: Another popular method of diversification is to choose investments from different countries. Typically, you would have varying degrees of exposure to the main market groups, such as America, Europe, and Asia, and an evolving group named the emerging markets.

- **Asset industry**: Given the humongous impact of tech stocks in recent decades, it makes sense to diversify into other more traditional industries when tech dominates many indexes, such as S&P 500 and NASDAQ-100. There is a plethora of dedicated funds for obvious and niche industries, from energy and consumer goods to biotech and robotics.

- **Currency**: While this would not have much impact on an American Robo-advisor operating in America, it is a more complex issue for markets with less stable currencies and low availability of local currency investment products. In certain cases, it may be necessary to combine US dollar products with locally denominated products to hedge against bias and volatility against the US dollar, especially if your income and spending are in local currency. Differences in taxation may also need to be addressed when choosing products.

- **Fees**: While not necessary for the purposes of diversification directly, commonly used criteria for product selection are fees. Some popular products such as ETFs start from a small fraction of 1 percent in annual fees, but certain mutual funds can have complicated fee schedules that also place limitations on how and when you can sell them for profit. Generally speaking, the tendency is to prefer high-volume, low-cost ETF providers.

To build our portfolios, we would feed in a selection of products using the factors listed previously. To construct a typical set of four to five Robo-advisor model portfolios, you would start from a product universe of 10–20 products. The more products you add, the more transactions you will potentially generate down the line, therefore generating more fees and overhead. Using the MPT calculations, we feed in our products and any assumptions to generate our efficient frontier.

Now, we can finally put everything together and combine our MPT and risk questionnaire. The intersection of these two is the efficient frontier we receive as an output from our MPT calculations. We need to split the efficient frontier along its path into segments called risk bands. Each risk band defines a portfolio that we can then map to different risk scores. The simplest case is that we have a risk score of 1–5 and five risk bands. Therefore, the investors with the lowest risk score of 1 will be allocated into risk band 1, which then becomes portfolio 1. Similarly, the investors with the highest appetite for risk would be allocated into risk band 5, and then portfolio 5.

Projections

A typical Robo-advisor workflow will include some type of projection once the portfolio allocation has been made. This highlights to the investor what outcomes are possible and probable, given their selections thus far. This becomes particularly interesting in the context of Goal-based investing, whereby we can now estimate the likelihood of achieving the intended Goal in the intended timeframe. There will be more on that in the next section.

There are a few popular methods to calculate these projections that are commonly used by Robo-advisors:

- **Probabilistic return**: We can use simple future value and compound interest calculations to understand the expected value of our portfolio, given its return and risk characteristics.

- **Monte-Carlo simulation**: A more exotic approach would be to introduce random variables into our expected return model to reflect the often chaotic nature of real-world financial markets. This method was developed by Manhattan Project mathematicians Stanislaw Ulam and John von Neumann, and is named after the famous Mediterranean casino town.

We will look at the specific formulas and implementation specifics of these methods in *Chapter 9, Investment Projections*.

Risk profiling and projections for Goals

If we weren't using Goal-based investment as our framework, then we'd be finished now and could move on to the next topic. However, Goals present a few additional opportunities when it comes to risk profiling and projections. One key decision to consider is whether to support a single Goal or multiple Goals. The difference becomes apparent when we consider risk profiling.

Suppose the question is around risk tolerance. Without the context of Goals, you would answer the questionnaire while considering all your savings and any plans and aspirations for the future. Yet if we were to consider answering in the context of individual Goals, those answers might look quite different. For example, you can easily imagine being comfortable with more risk for a Goal with a time span of several decades, especially if it represents something aspirational, such as buying a holiday home or yacht to enjoy retirement. Contrast that with something shorter term that has a fixed timeline and little flexibility, such as getting married next year or a child about to enter college.

Goal-based investing, therefore, offers us the unique ability to consider risk tolerance separately for each Goal. The implication is that we may well end up with different risk scores, resulting in different portfolio allocations. This is something we will need to consider when we decide how to structure accounts.

A further opportunity unique to Goal-based investing is that of Goal probability. Even a traditional projection chart becomes more useful through the specific lens of Goal-based investing. The target amount and time span are no longer abstract or even random choices. Goals give meaning to these choices. When are you getting married? How much is the dress, ring, or venue? You quickly see how Goals transform discussions about investing into discussions about life choices. When we consider factors such as average returns and variance, the resulting projection also allows us to sample the distribution. Then, we can ask questions such as how likely we are to achieve the target amount within the investment time span – that is, your Goal probability.

These metrics are now hard, deterministic answers about the future. They are, however, useful metrics to consider what risk and volatility in outcomes you are willing to accept in the context of a specific Goal. This context makes it easier to think about scenarios in real-life terms. Am I comfortable with a 50% chance of missing my target? Can I delay retirement by 2–3 years? Can I buy my dream house with 70% of the budget? Ultimately, these are the questions that will help investors make informed decisions about their money, and that is the true benefit of Goal-based investing.

At this point in the workflow, we have our complete investment plan. We know how much money we are investing, what for, over what time period, and into which portfolio. Now, it's time to make that plan a reality.

Opening accounts, performing KYC and AML, and funding accounts

The first step of bringing our plan to life is to open an investment account where your money will be placed and, once investments have been made, where any investment products will be held.

Investment accounts are just like bank accounts, but in addition to holding cash, they can hold various types of investments. Financial institutions providing such investment accounts are called custodians. While many banks are also custodians, there are many specialists that provide such services, including some online brokers and even a few Robo-advisors. Generally speaking, the complexities of custody are not part of this book, so we will assume a third-party custodian to manage our accounts. For the sake of simplicity, we will assume our broker and custodian are one and the same financial institution.

Automated account opening

As we established in *Chapter 1, Introduction to Robo-Advisors*, a key consideration for any Robo-advisor is convenience. Generally speaking, there should no longer be a need for any physical paperwork of any kind. This has been a rapid transformation of the industry, as a mere decade ago, physical paperwork and wet signatures were the industry norm. Luckily, regulators in most countries have adopted standards for electronic forms and digital signatures to facilitate financial transactions.

In the context of a Robo-advisor, we will be providing answers to a specific list of questions relating to the account opening standards at the custodian. The exact contents and structure of those questions vary and are not standardized, but are largely driven by KYC and AML requirements. In practice, this means we will need to provide facilities for investors to populate a series of digital forms, and then provide digital signatures for those forms to be filed with the custodian. This filing can take place via a simple email, a file transfer facility, or, in most cases today, an **Application Programming Interface (API)**, which allows our software to pass the data directly to the recipient software for immediate processing.

Due to the popularity of online stock trading in recent years, great advances have been made in automating this process. In many developed countries, you can expect a largely automated process that will either result in access to an account in just a few minutes when fully automated or, at worst, a few days of waiting time for some limited human review and approvals of your account information.

Different types of accounts

For the purposes of this book, we will assume the simplest form of investment account with no special features, which is the individual investment account. However, it is worth noting that in many countries, there are a whole host of specialized account types that are designed for different investment scenarios. The obvious one is a joint account between spouses.

In countries that have taxes on investments or offer government pension plans, there is often a need for some form of retirement account. America has the 401(k) and **Individual Retirement Account (IRA)**, Australia has its superannuation, and Singapore has its **Central Provident Fund (CPF)**. All of these are local forms of retirement accounts. In practice, the idea is to offer tax incentives for keeping money locked away until retirement and tax penalties for taking money out early. In many cases, these retirement accounts also have limits on how much money can be contributed over a calendar year or a lifetime, and whether the money comes from the individual and/or employer.

There is also the question of structuring accounts between investors. To begin with, you could just have one individual account for each investor, and then trade and report on them individually. In practice, when dealing with large numbers of investors and accounts, it starts to make more sense to aggregate these under one master or omnibus account. This means that all trades are made in one large account and then allocated back to individual subaccounts. This often makes trading faster and more cost-efficient but does introduce complexities, to the implementation and order management in particular. Again, local regulations will determine what is both possible and cost-efficient.

We will leave these complexities outside the scope of this book, but it is worth noting that these specialized account types will play an increasingly important role as Robo-advisors expand the scope of services and financial planning tools they provide.

Accounting for Goals

One further complication to factor in is Goals. Most early Robo-advisors only supported one account type, and each investor was allocated their own individual investment account. That kept account opening, reporting, and statements very neat and tidy. Once Goals were introduced, they presented a challenge. Do you lump together multiple Goals into one investment account, split them so that each Goal has its own account, or introduce some further subaccount structure? There are many technical and practical considerations when choosing a strategy, but for the sake of simplicity, we will assume different accounts for different Goals.

KYC and AML

You may have read stories about how criminals or corporations have pulled off money laundering schemes, and the solution to that problem has been KYC and AML. While distinctly separate processes, they are ultimately aiming at the same thing – making sure you really know who the investor is and where this money is coming from.

The local regulations and reporting requirements for KYC and AML will vary, but broadly speaking, you need to prove two things – an identity for KYC and a source of funds for AML. The former sounds more commonplace, but many countries do not have digital identity services available, making the process more difficult to automate. Where national identity services are available, it might be a case of providing a social security number or logging in via a government-controlled identity platform. In other cases, you may need to ask the investor to upload proof of identity in the form of a passport and possibly some form of proof of address, such as a recent utility bill.

For AML purposes, it starts with a simple question of where the cash for investing is coming from. Further, while ultimately each Robo-advisor is responsible and accountable for which clients they accept, there are platforms that offer checks against global databases of known criminals and terrorists.

Funding your account

Now that we have opened an account, the next logical step is to put some money into it. Traditionally, the obvious way to do this is by wire transfer. All you would need to provide the investor is their account number and wire instructions provided by the custodian. The obvious downside to this is that, in many cases, it may take several days for the money to show up in your account, ready to invest. This doesn't feel very convenient. Further, as a complication for the Robo-advisor, that process is not in your control and must be done entirely outside your platform. The investor would need to use their own online banking provider and enter all information manually, including the right amount.

To facilitate a smoother, faster process, many countries offer facilities for direct debit. For our Robo-advisor, this means we can request money directly from the investor's bank, obviously with the investor's approval and proper credentials. In America, this direct debit scheme is called **Automated Clearing House** (**ACH**) transfers. Plaid, a popular fintech provider, offers an API and tools to enable ACH transfers for any platform needing direct debit transfers. Similar solutions exist in other countries but are not yet widespread. This approach offers the ultimate convenience, as the entire experience happens within your Robo-advisor platform – yes, even the step of providing online banking credentials. The security of such a transaction is managed by Plaid, which is simply embedded into your Robo-advisor through a widget.

In America, in addition to cash transfers, it is also possible to transfer existing positions using another scheme called **Automated Customer Account Transfer Service** (**ACATS**). This is relevant to Robo-advisors as it enables investors to utilize existing online brokerage accounts to fund new investments in your Robo-advisor. However, since this is specific to America and not an essential core feature, it is not within the scope of this book.

Now that we've set up and funded our accounts, it's time to make our first transaction and place an order to buy an investment product.

Introducing order management and execution

Up to this point, all we have done is set the stage for the main task of a Robo-advisor – to make investments. In one sense, it sounds quite simple. We simply make an order and send it to a broker who executes that order – kind of like ordering food in a restaurant. In reality, it is more complicated, as there are a lot of moving parts involved when we wish to automate the entire process. We will break down the steps involved in the next few sections.

Price feed

Before we can place an order, it seems logical that we would need a price list, just like a menu at a restaurant. In finance, we call this a price feed. For the specific needs of a Robo-advisor, our needs are rather simple compared to real-time stock trading or advanced institutional trading. All we really need is a list of products and a single price for each day. The reason for this is that we will be executing our trades only once per day, not in real time. This ensures that all customers and all orders receive the same price, and we can take advantage of larger trading blocks to reduce our trading costs. Luckily for us, such simple data feeds can be found free of charge via online APIs such as Yahoo Finance, which is what we will be using in our hands-on work.

Broker

Once we know a price, we need a place to send our order. This is called a **broker**. A broker is a type of financial institution that deals with making transactions in financial markets. There are various types of brokers for various purposes, but the needs of a Robo-advisor are quite basic. One important factor to consider is that for the sake of automation, we require some type of programmatic interface to send our orders and receive updates about their status. Your two choices are batch file transfer or some type of API. The former means your platform must compile orders into a file, such as a spreadsheet, to be digested by the broker's systems. The latter means you pass batches of orders directly from your software into theirs.

Compliance

Before we can go ahead and generate orders and send them across to our broker, we need to confirm a few things. The job of compliance is to ensure we stick to regulations and generally good practices in how we operate our business. For example, we want to ensure that orders generated by investors are valid – that is, we don't want to sell assets we don't own, and we want to avoid buying assets with money we don't have in our account.

Order management

When we think about creating an order with our broker, we have to remember that they operate at the product level. The broker doesn't take orders for portfolios, let alone Goals. They will expect line items by investment product, of how many units or dollars' worth of each product we are looking to purchase. Therefore, the job of our order management must be to translate, or split, what our investors have created on our platform into bite-size chunks that a broker can process. When dealing with omnibus accounts, we would further need to aggregate orders from individual accounts into the master account. Besides new Goals or accounts created by investors, we can also include orders coming from rebalancing, which we will cover further in the chapter.

Order execution

The process of order execution is like the post office sending out its mail in a truck. We have received orders from investors, made sure they are valid, and are now ready to pass them along to the broker for execution.

Order allocation

Once we receive responses for our order, we need to reverse the process to ensure that all our investor accounts and Goals are updated to reflect the exact prices when orders were executed.

This concludes the core features needed to set up a Robo-advisor. There are still a few key pieces required to keep it running, which we will now dive into.

Learning how to operate a Robo-advisor

Once you have your Robo-advisor up and running with investors and funded accounts, there are a number of operational processes to take care of. Some of these require daily actions, while others are more infrequent. Many of these processes can once again be automated, but certain human oversight is necessary, due to potential complications and exceptions that may happen when dealing with human investors. We will explore these in the following sections. The following chart breaks down the key processes we will need to cover.

Standard Robo-Advisor Operations

Dividends	Rebalancing	Reporting	Statements	Client Management	Fee Management	Monitoring

Figure 2.2 – The standard operations for a Robo-advisor

Dividends

A rather pesky feature of many investment products is that underneath a fund structure such as an ETF, there are actual company stocks. According to law, these companies must report and pay out any dividends decided by the board of directors quarterly. Therefore, if your portfolio contains the stocks of these companies, then we must factor in and pay out such dividends over time. Luckily, in the case of ETFs such as the S&P 500, we don't need to calculate that for all 500 companies separately; that is partly why we pay a premium to the manager of the ETF product. Nevertheless, some portfolios may include up to dozens of different ETFs, so these must be tallied up and paid out in cash or accumulated into the holdings of each account. Depending on the type of products and funds used, this may be a major component of the investment thesis, especially when it relates to fixed-income products such as bonds.

Fee management and billing

If you're building a Robo-advisor just to manage your own money, then you won't be needing to bill yourself for using your own platform. However, if you're building a platform for investors, then billing will be your main source of revenue and rather important. While the most common form of platform fee is charged as an annual percentage of assets managed, some platforms choose to offer flat subscription fees instead. The rationale is that most retail investors are not used to prices in basis points but are fine with paying $10 a month in subscription fees for Spotify or Netflix.

You may also need to consider a host of other fees imposed on you by the broker and/or custodian. These might include account opening, management, or transaction fees, all of which must be deducted from investor accounts in some way. Depending on the account structures available to you, it may be as simple as withdrawing an amount for the fees in cash. In many cases, you may need to force-sell one or more units of a product to generate enough cash for those fees.

Rebalancing

One of the biggest party tricks of a Robo-advisor is the ability to automate rebalancing, which was a cumbersome process in the old days. Rebalancing is really what it sounds like. As financial markets move up and down, the various constituents of your portfolios will do the same. Depending on market conditions, stocks and bonds might move either in unison or in opposite directions. In the latter case, what can happen is that the value of stocks in your portfolio can dramatically shift, which happened during the COVID-19 pandemic years of 2020 and 2021.

The challenge with this is that a conservative portfolio with just 20% of its value in stocks may have now shifted to 50% or more in stocks. This implies that you are taking more risks than you had intended. Therefore, the logical thing to do is to sell some of those stock holdings and use the proceeds to buy more bonds back for your portfolio. That series of transactions would rebalance the portfolio back to the original ratio of 20% stocks and 80% bonds.

To implement rebalancing, we would need an automated report to identify accounts, Goals, and portfolios that have drifted far from their intended models. This can either be done periodically, with quarterly being the most popular choice, or by threshold. The latter option means we simply pick an acceptable percentage of drift compared to the model, and if this threshold is exceeded, we trigger orders to rebalance the portfolio.

One final trick we have up our sleeves is tax optimization. While not applicable to all countries and use cases, the original American Robo-advisor comes with tax-loss harvesting. This is a mechanism specific to American tax laws, whereby you can offset your capital gains taxes by selling loss-making positions. The beauty of automation means we can run these reports and take advantage of this opportunity with the click of a button.

Performance reporting

While we have already covered performance calculations in projections when creating new portfolios, we also need to consider the ongoing duty of maintaining performance reports. By law, investors should be able to access their accounts whenever they want and find performance numbers for their portfolios. This ensures there is no misunderstanding about how investments are performing, especially in times of uncertainty and market turbulence. In most cases, the diversification built into our portfolios should comfort investors in that the exposure to individual volatile assets is limited, and offset by performance across asset classes, geographies, and industries.

The two main methodologies for calculating profit and loss are as follows:

- **Time-Weighted Rate of Return** (**TWRR**): The simplest method of projecting potential portfolio returns; this approach ignores any additional money coming in or out of your portfolio. It's like putting aside an existing nest egg for a number of years to see what happens.

- **Money-Weighted Rate of Return** (**MWRR**): This is a more sophisticated version of TWRR, whereby we factor in cash flows going in and out of our investment. This is particularly important for a Robo-advisor that supports monthly deposits into your portfolio or Goals. Over long periods of time, the monthly deposits quickly become the largest factor in overall returns.

Statements

Another piece of the operational puzzle is statements, in particular regulatory statements such as annual filings and tax statements. Oftentimes, most of these can be sourced from your broker and custodian, ideally via some automated interface whereby you can retrieve them. Alternatively, they can be sent directly to investors via email, based on their accounts at the custodian.

Account and user management

Lastly, a big part of operating a Robo-advisor is the human investors. Well, that is assuming you have included a CAPTCHA challenge as part of your onboarding to keep away the bots! Humans have needs, questions, and concerns. In the case of a Robo-advisor, you are a service provider and must cater to these needs, exacerbated by the fact that money is involved. You may also be contacted by third parties such as government agencies and will need granular administrative control over all accounts to suspend, activate, or close them as required. Over time, you will also need to comply with regulations around document storage, including changes to identity or proof-of-address documents. You may need to introduce further automation to ensure investors confirm their KYC and AML information on an annual basis.

Summary

We covered a lot of ground in this chapter, introducing a plethora of new concepts and terminology. First, we built a profile of a user with simple financial planning questions. From there, we used Markowitz's MPT framework to build risk profiles and portfolios. We looked at how to open accounts to hold our money and investments. We defined the basic types of transactions we will need for our Robo-advisor. Finally, we established the core processes needed to run an operational Robo-advisor.

This will serve as a nice overview if you get lost in the details later on in the book, so feel free to bookmark this for later reference. You should now have a high-level grasp of the task ahead, as we get closer to building our own Robo-advisor, putting together all the elements we've introduced in this chapter.

In the next chapter, we will consider two approaches to putting these pieces together – either building a set of algorithms to use piecemeal or building a platform with a user interface, allowing for mass consumption of our Robo-advisor.

Further reading

You might be interested in reading some extra information related to the topics discussed in this chapter. Here is a link to an external resource:

- Markowitz, Harry. Portfolio Selection. *The Journal of Finance*, vol. 7, no. 1, 1952, pp. 77–91: `https://www.jstor.org/stable/2975974`.

Robo-Advisor Platforms versus Algorithms

Before we start building a Robo-advisor, we should explore two different scenarios you might be considering. First, we'll discuss setting up a series of algorithms to help manage your own investments. Second, we'll evaluate building up a complete platform that can serve other investors. These two scenarios are fundamentally totally different strategies, the latter implying setting up and registering a company with regulated operations.

In this chapter, we will take a peek at some of the key algorithms that we will get some hands-on practice with later in this book. Then we will cover the means of scaling such algorithms for use with customers. Finally, we will discuss the additional requirements involved in setting up a commercial Robo-advisor as a business.

In this chapter, we're going to cover the following topics:

- Managing your own investments with Robo-advisor algorithms
- Managing customer investments with a Robo-advisor platform
- Scaling up from algorithms to a full Robo-advisor platform

Managing your own investments with Robo-advisor algorithms

The algorithms that power a Robo-advisor are its essence. After all, automation is the reason for its existence. Without automation, you could certainly carry out all the necessary calculations on a spreadsheet, just like any financial advisor would. Using what we learned in the previous chapter, the main algorithms required to run a Robo-advisor are as follows:

- **Goal creation** (**for Goal-based investing**): Optional, but helpful to capture basic information about the investment such as the target amount, time horizon, initial investment, and monthly deposits. We'll be covering this in *Chapter 6*. Our intention is to create a reusable class of objects that allows us to create Goals and use their stored information with other algorithms. An example would be the following:

```
myGoal = Goal("Retirement",
                targetYear=2060,
                targetValue=3000000)
```

- **Risk questionnaire**: A set of questions you could define yourself, but preferably will source from government-mandated questionnaires or industry best practices. We'll be covering this in *Chapter 7*. Our intention is to create interactive questionnaires that can be read from a file and generate a risk score.

```
questionsFileName = '/content/drive/MyDrive/Books/Robo-advisor with Python /Data/Risk Questions.csv'
answersFileName = '/content/drive/MyDrive/Books/Robo-advisor with Python /Data/Risk Answers.csv'

toleranceQuestionnaire = RiskQuestionnaire()
toleranceQuestionnaire.loadQuestionnaire(questionsFileName, answersFileName, "Tolerance")

capacityQuestionnaire = RiskQuestionnaire()
capacityQuestionnaire.loadQuestionnaire(questionsFileName, answersFileName, "Capacity")

toleranceQuestionnaire.answerQuestionnaire()
capacityQuestionnaire.answerQuestionnaire()
```

```
In general, how would your best friend describe you as a risk taker?
0: A real gambler
1: Willing to take risks after completing adequate research
2: Cautious
3: A real risk avoider
Choose your answer between 0 and 3: 
```

Figure 3.1 – Example of running an interactive questionnaire

- **Risk score**: A calculator to rate your risk questionnaire answers and combine results for risk tolerance and risk capacity into a single score. We'll be covering this in *Chapter 7*.

- **Portfolio construction**: A set of model portfolios constructed from available products at your chosen broker using MPT calculations. We'll be covering this in *Chapter 8*. We will be building a set of tools to model, create, and analyze portfolios. Here is an example of an output we will generate:

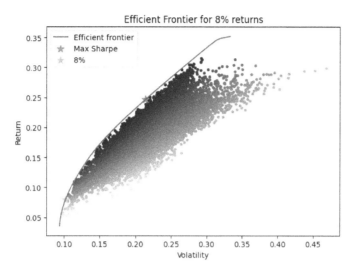

Figure 3.2 – An example output we will create for our portfolio

- **Portfolio allocation**: A matrix of allocating risk scores to your model portfolios. We'll be covering this in *Chapter 8*. This will combine outputs of risk scores and portfolio construction.

- **Projections**: A calculator to estimate and/or visualize future investment outcomes. We'll be covering this in *Chapter 9*. We will implement simple calculations to generate probable future outcomes for our portfolios, using visualizations like this:

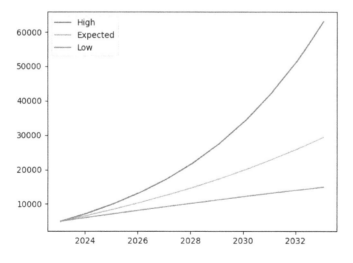

Figure 3.3 – Example projection chart

- **Order management**: A calculator to produce a series of orders based on the preceding outputs. We'll be covering this in *Chapter 12*. This will be the most complicated part of the book, as we will need to manage the various objects we create between Goals, portfolios, and accounts. We will be generating and manipulating orders as in the following example:

	A	B	C	D
1		Symbol	Type	DollarAmount
2	0	GLD	BUY	11.1015
3	1	IEI	BUY	6.159
4	2	TLT	BUY	2.4336
5	3	VTI	BUY	10.3059

Figure 3.4 – Example order file

- **Rebalancing**: A calculator to determine whether any drift from the model is present in your portfolio, and which orders need to be rebalanced. We'll be covering this in *Chapter 14*. This algorithm will help us return portfolio allocations to their intended proportions by generating the necessary buy and sell orders using our work from *Chapter 12*.

You will not need many of the elements we covered in the previous chapter, because you will not be onboarding any other investors besides yourself. Therefore, you could run your algorithms without the need for a user interface, potentially, and just take outputs from the command line or as simple spreadsheets.

Beyond the algorithms, you would still need to interact with at least one financial institution that provides you with brokerage and custody services. Firstly, you would need to manually open one or more accounts and perform KYC and AML checks as required. You could use your algorithms only to generate orders offline and then place those orders manually via a user interface from your online broker. This would be the easiest and fastest implementation.

If you are indeed aiming to fully automate these transactions, it is not enough to have access to an online dashboard or mobile app. Beyond the core algorithms listed, you would need to implement fully automated order management including order allocation and aggregation, which is very complicated. Your Robo-advisor will require programmatic access, nowadays typically via an API. There are dedicated providers for such services, but they're not available from your local bank. This seems unnecessarily complicated for the purpose of managing your own investments.

Now let's up the ante and consider what it would take to let other people use our Robo-advisor.

Managing customer investments with Robo-advisor platforms

The word algorithm implies capabilities that exist in code only. If you wish to use them, you need to have access to that code. A platform, on the other hand, implies there is some additional surrounding technology in place to enable other people or technologies to interact with your algorithms.

In the context of Robo-advisors, your obvious candidates for a platform would be the following:

- **API**: If you're building a Robo-advisor platform, then you will need an API in any scenario. That's because an app or website will need to communicate with your algorithms, and the way to do that is via an API. If your plan is to serve other businesses instead of consumers, then you could stop here and simply license your algorithms via an API, charging a fraction of a cent each time they are called.

- **Mobile app**: Most direct-to-consumer Robo-advisor platforms these days opt to engage their customers primarily through an app. The obvious benefit is that it's always in your pocket, you can reach investors via notifications, and can take advantage of on-device capabilities such as the camera for scanning documents and face- or fingerprint-based multi-factor authentication for additional security.

- **Website**: The obvious thing to do would be to serve up your Robo-advisor as a traditional website, albeit ideally optimized for mobile consumption. It would be cheaper and faster than building an app that needs to work for Apple and Android ecosystems.

Let's now proceed to review what it would take to move from algorithms to these platform strategies.

Scaling up from algorithms to a full Robo-advisor platform

The biggest difference in transitioning from some algorithms to a platform is not the technology but the people. Operating a platform that accepts other investors' money is also a business, and will be regulated as such by your local government.

I'm not a lawyer, so I can't give you a specific list of requirements as they will depend on your location and be subject to ongoing revision by regulators. However, here are some common concerns that you will need to address in order to serve investors with your platform:

- **Tech team**: If you are a developer, you have the ability to write your own algorithms. However, is it realistic for you to build the necessary backend services to publish your own APIs? Can you also build a website and/or apps? In reality, you're going to need a tech team with experience in financial services. Your partners will expect an experienced team to interact with, who are familiar with industry standards and procedures, especially around security and testing. You would ideally fill positions for a head of design, backend lead, frontend lead, QA lead, and head of security, complemented by additional developers or contractors as needed.

- **Regulatory licensing**: Before being allowed to place your first trade, you will be expected to seek regulatory approval for operating a Robo-advisor in your country. Some developed markets have quite clear processes and guidelines in place, while many do not. This means this process is likely to be exploratory in nature and can take many months and hefty legal fees to complete. Depending on your situation, as advised by your legal team, you may be required to apply for capital markets, fund management, or advisory licensing, or a combination of these options. Often, as part of these approvals, there will be an audit of your platform, team, and business model, so you can't expect to go in with a PowerPoint and walk out with a stamped scroll in hand.

- **Capital requirements**: Another important factor in regulatory oversight is sufficient capital. Generally speaking, regulators frown upon anyone operating in their jurisdiction on shaky ground. While it may seem unnecessary at first, when the markets get choppy and investors scramble to liquidate their portfolios, regulators want to avoid the all-out chaos of operators finding themselves fresh out of liquidity. The requirements will vary and are subject to change but expect to walk in with a seven-figure bag of coins or risk being sent packing.

- **Broker and custodian**: To keep things simple, you would find one partner that provides both services. Typically, a bank or online broker will provide custodial services either themselves or through an established partner. You will need to agree on pricing, and go through their certification process for integration. This means you need a working platform before you can properly engage with a broker. Keep in mind that brokers' fee models will vary wildly, and some may impose minimum balances and fees that you must account for in your own business plan.

- **Certified expertise and experience**: While, technically, anyone with some Python skills could build a Robo-advisor, it doesn't mean that they will be allowed to operate one in public. The expectations often focus on the main roles of such a company – the chief executive officer and chief investment officer. Regulators will expect proof of expertise and sufficient experience in operating in capital markets.

- **Compliance**: Your team will need to appoint a compliance officer, and have the staff on hand to ensure the proper process is followed, especially in KYC and AML procedures – because, at the end of the day, your company is responsible for ensuring no bad actors end up as clients.

- **Marketing**: Assuming you've cleared the preceding hurdles with flying colors, your next problem will be finding customers. In developed countries, the Robo-advisor market may have already become rather saturated. You will be competing against venture capital-backed start-ups and well-known financial institutions including banks, asset managers, and wealth managers. All of them will be competing for the same top spot in the Google search results and social media engagement. You will need the expertise to find ways to differentiate yourself from the crowd, and more importantly, budget to compete. Marketing isn't cheap, and spending must be consistent to achieve results.

- **Customer service**: Finally, once you have new investors as your customers, they will expect to reach you via online chat, email, phone, and possibly in person. You will need all the systems and trained staff in place from day one to answer questions about how to use your platform, but also why certain products are or aren't in your portfolio, why their risk score is so low/high, how you justify your outlandish fees, and why your funds are underperforming a certain index or fund compared to their other advisor. While a Robo-advisor is designed to be automated, many Robo-advisors choose to employ licensed financial advisors, in part to help investors navigate all these questions and bring them the peace of mind that is harder to achieve with technology alone.

If you're setting out to tinker with some algorithms to manage your Excel portfolio, you can steam right ahead and you'll have everything you need in this book alone.

However, if you're intending to serve the public with a new Robo-advisor platform, you have a whole lot of work ahead of you beyond the scope we will cover in the remainder of this book. I can help you put together the core capabilities and algorithms of your platform, but the rest is up to you.

Summary

This chapter served as a fork in the road for you, depending on your intentions and background. For those interested in running their own Robo-advisor algorithms on a home laptop, we listed the main algorithms you'll be building through this book. We also highlighted the extensive resources, capital, and skills required for those seeking to build commercial platforms.

The next chapter will be of particular interest to those planning on building platforms and will help you decide how much of the entire system you should build, buy, or lease. Whichever strategy is appropriate for your plans, you'll find guidance for the core algorithms in *Part 2* of this book.

4

Leasing, Buying, or Building Your Own Robo-Advisor

In this final chapter of *Part 1*, we will close out the strategic portion of this book to consider why you are planning to build your own Robo-advisor. This decision will have different criteria depending on whether you are an individual investor looking to manage your own money or a business looking to offer digital wealth services to customers.

In the previous chapter, we established the requirements you would face for either scenario. What remains is to look at the alternatives and weigh the pros and cons to determine the right path for you. In this chapter, we will explore the three strategies of leasing, buying, or building a Robo-advisor. While this breakdown may not be exhaustive and complete, it is based on real-world experiences from working with Bambu clients around the world.

By the end of the chapter, you should have a better understanding of the criteria involved in choosing the right strategy for your Robo-advisor.

In this chapter, we're going to cover the following topics:

- Building or subscribing to a Robo-advisor as a consumer
- Building, buying, or leasing a Robo-advisor platform as a business

Building or subscribing to a Robo-advisor as a consumer

As discussed in the previous chapter, building a Robo-advisor for your own personal use is quite a project. Besides knowledge and skill in programming, which we will explore in detail in the next chapter, you need a good reason to spend all that time building something you could also find online. Therefore, let's explore reasons you might choose either path.

Here are some reasons you might choose to build your own Robo-advisor:

- You're interested in algorithmic trading and would enjoy the process of implementing your own Robo-advisor algorithms

- You're considering a career in digital wealth and consider it a learning opportunity

- You're considering starting a digital wealth business and are exploring the feasibility of building a platform by exploring the underlying algorithms first

- You don't have access to a Robo-advisor or are prohibited from using them

Certainly, this is not an exhaustive list. These are simply some obvious reasons you might choose to pursue a Robo-advisor of your own. While I do invite all readers to continue along and finish the rest of this book, there is no obligation to start programming your own Robo-advisor. You might simply be curious to learn how these systems work for pure intellectual delight.

Let's establish reasons you would wish to subscribe to an existing Robo-advisor, instead of building your own:

- You don't have the time to build a Robo-advisor

- You are only managing your own money

- You don't have access to an online broker API

- You don't want to build and manage your own portfolios

Again, these do not prevent you from reading on. The learnings from this book can be applied in many ways, without necessitating a full implementation. You can also explore specific topics such as **rebalancing** individually if that is of particular interest to you.

Now let's switch gears to look at another use case for businesses.

Building, buying, or leasing a Robo-advisor platform as a business

Robo-advisors have become something of a *hygiene* product in the financial markets of developed countries. This means customers of the main financial institutions such as banks and online brokers expect a Robo-advisor capability as part of the available product suite. This adoption has been going on globally for the last 5 years. Adoption has been faster in major financial markets and is gradually trickling down to lower tiers and smaller markets.

It isn't uncommon in 2023 to see smaller financial institutions such as credit unions or regional banks in large financial markets developing Robo-advisor solutions. Similarly, the main banks of niche markets and smaller developing countries are engaging in similar initiatives.

All of these companies must go through the same decision-making process: build, buy, or lease. Certainly, the big players in big markets went through this exercise years ago, mostly aided by expensive management consultants and extensive market research. However, none of these decisions are forever. Many large institutions have engaged in multiple different strategies across their various segments and markets, buying in some and leasing or building in others.

Let's start by exploring why most companies choose to lease a Robo-advisor solution.

Leasing a Robo-advisor

Here are some common reasons why companies might choose leasing as the best option:

- They don't have the time and/or budget to build a Robo-advisor
- They aren't sure about their digital wealth strategy yet
- They don't have the skills and maturity to embark on a complex digital implementation
- They don't have a clear product vision for their own Robo-advisor
- They wish to benefit from the shared research and development costs of a ready-made platform
- Their requirements are fairly standard or flexible
- They are in a rush to get into the market with a Robo-advisor solution

Since most companies will adopt this approach, we should expand on a few key topics here in more depth. After all, these may be key questions you are considering at your company right now.

Calculating the time and money required to build a Robo-advisor

At the end of the day, time and money are what businesses measure when they consider any investment or project. If you're in a competitive market, and already late to the game, can you afford to establish a team in-house?

For sure, starting from scratch, we are talking about it taking at least 2 years to build a Robo-advisor platform. In that time, you will not be launching anything new or interesting, just a basic vanilla implementation without any bells and whistles. I've seen large banks spend more than 6 months debating how to visualize a performance chart. That's just one part of one screen of a Robo-advisor. Large institutions also come with large legacy systems that necessitate lengthy integration projects. A transactional integration to a core banking system could alone take 12–18 months. Adding other platforms for **Know Your Customer** (**KYC**), **Customer Relationship Management** (**CRM**), and **Anti-Money Laundering** (**AML**) will each add months.

In plain terms, all of this is going to be very, very expensive. In my experience, you will need the core team to be in-house employees, not cheap overseas contractors. That's because the knowledge built around how the Robo-advisor works will be built over years and become critical to later development and innovation. A minimum project team for the core Robo-advisor build with a project manager(s), subject matter expert(s), product owner(s), scrum master(s), UX designer(s), UI designer(s), solution architect(s), frontend developers, backend developers, and an infrastructure team will quickly run past 20 **Full-time Equivalent (FTE)**. That's even before you consider sales, marketing, and customer support when live. On an average salary of $100,000 across those roles, you're looking at an annual run rate of a minimum of $2 million.

So, the question becomes how clear is your vision for your Robo-advisor? Are you willing to invest millions of dollars and several years to get into the marketplace? If the answer isn't a resounding yes, then you should consider leasing or licensing a platform instead. For most financial institutions, these kinds of budgets are way out of their league.

When it comes to finding a ready-made platform, there are some further alternatives, which we will break down next.

Leasing versus licensing a Robo-advisor

Leasing tends to imply the usage of a ready-made product or service. In the case of Robo-advisors, leasing implies **Software-as-a-Service (SaaS)**. In other use cases, most SaaS platforms emerge once a new innovative service has been on the market for years. This is because SaaS necessitates an extreme standardization of requirements. If every client has different requirements, you need the ability to customize some of the code per client. This is not possible with a SaaS platform. Due to the relative novelty, diversity in requirements across market segments, and the inherent complexity of Robo-advisors, we have not seen many attempts at a full SaaS model yet.

The clear alternative to a SaaS platform is licensing, which implies some form of **Customized Off-The-Shelf (COTS)** solution. This can take the form of a Robo-advisor API, or simply a company that will build you your own Robo-advisor from ready-made modules, kind of like a piece of IKEA furniture. Much like SaaS, the API model has not yet taken hold in the B2B market for Robo-advisor solutions. Most companies looking to build a Robo-advisor do not have the digital maturity and experience to consume a set of APIs. Therefore, the dominant form of licensing remains a custom build.

Here is an example from Bambu of what a typical API library would look like. Such websites provide detailed documentation about how to consume the APIs on offer.

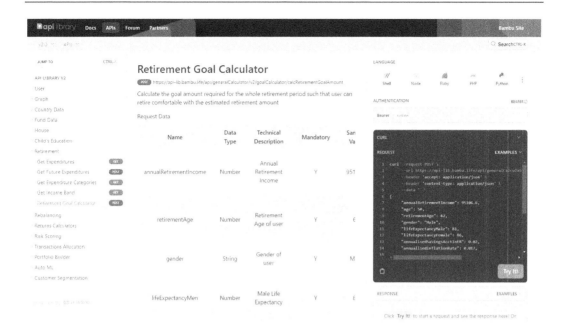

Figure 4.1 – Example of an API library by Bambu

Many other segments within fintech have already adopted APIs to a large extent. Some of the largest fintech start-ups in the world offer only one product: a payment API. However, it may take years for other more traditional fintech use cases such as wealth management to adopt an API-first approach to building solutions.

The approach of a custom build is a natural halfway house between building from scratch and leasing something off the shelf. There is a gray area of flexibility there in terms of strategy and requirements, and many different providers have specialized in individual markets or segments. Therefore, financial institutions can benefit from the learnings, skills, and capabilities built around their own customer base.

Similarly, there is a wide range of offerings to accommodate various levels of budgets, which typically correspond to complexity and flexibility in requirements. For example, most large institutions would insist on a fully customized digital user experience, often integrated into existing online and mobile channels. Conversely, a small advisory group may be happy to use an off-the-shelf website as long as they can put their logo on it. Likewise, there are similar differences in customization requirements for things such as broker integrations, products and portfolios, and rebalancing. The costliest items would be custom integrations into legacy transactional systems, which have to be built and tested extensively.

Generally, the more rigid your requirements, the larger the budget. Enterprise-grade solution providers will specialize in the high end of the market, often serving the largest wealth managers and banks for seven-figure multi-year contracts. Still, that may often represent massive savings when compared to embarking on a full in-house build at an enterprise scale.

This explains why very few financial institutions have taken on the burden of a full Robo-advisor build. However, there might be strategic reasons that leasing or licensing is not the right fit. Let's explore an alternative to buying a ready-made platform.

Buying a Robo-advisor

This is unlikely to be the strategy of choice for most businesses, due to the capital requirements involved. However, there might be special circumstances whereby the appeal of this approach might become relevant.

Here are some reasons why companies might choose to buy a Robo-advisor:

- You have a lot of capital but not enough time to build one
- There is a Robo-advisor threatening your market share
- You are in a beneficial capital position to consolidate your market share
- You have a tactical opportunity to acquire key Robo-advisor assets
- You're in a rush and need a market-leading Robo-advisor offering
- You consider it a strategic investment to own rather than build
- You're already invested in or commercially partnering with a Robo-advisor

Initially, when Robo-advisors started gaining traction in a few key markets, there was quite a lot of chatter about the large players jumping in to acquire the leading B2C contenders. Ultimately, that never quite happened as expected. Most of the successful B2C platforms are still operating independently, given the relative abundance of venture capital in recent years. The dream of a smashing IPO entry isn't dulled by the opportunity of a lower-value trade sale.

Despite all the focus on the marquee names on both sides of the rare mega deal, there is an undercurrent of natural consolidation happening. There have been hundreds, if not thousands of Robo-advisor start-ups over the past decade. Most of them will no longer be in operation for a variety of reasons. For example, even a smaller operating financial institution might choose to snag up a struggling B2C Robo-advisor. Even if the Robo-advisor does not come with a swath of users and assets, it may offer key enablers to jumpstart their own service in the form of a regulatory operating license or core technologies along with an experienced team.

If no other option fits the bill, you will need to build your own Robo-advisor. Let's dive into the thought process around this most challenging of options.

Building a Robo-advisor

Let's assume for the moment that you believe this is the right path for your business. In my experience, there are only a few special cases where this is genuinely the right path. Most businesses should really reconsider their reasons and try leasing, licensing, or buying instead.

Nevertheless, let's list some reasons why building a Robo-advisor might be attractive:

- You grossly underestimate the complexity, budget, or time required to build one

- You have a large budget, a clear vision, and very unique requirements

- You are starting your own Robo-advisor start-up and need to own the IP

- Your boss told you to build a Robo-advisor, so you bought this book

Oftentimes, we at Bambu see large financial institutions start with building a Robo-advisor as their working assumption. Typically, these companies already have decades of experience in building up their own digital channels across online banking or trading. To them, they see Robo-advisory as a natural extension of those capabilities. More often than not, this idea and strategy will be reversed after some months or years of wasted effort with little to show for it. Why is it so hard to get it right? Let me share some experiences.

Why building a Robo-advisor is really hard

The main reason I know it's hard is because I've done it. It took Bambu probably 3 years to get to a set of stable core capabilities, and that work continues to this day. No digital product is ever finished, and the pressure from the marketplace to keep innovating is relentless. Bambu is also in a somewhat unique position in that we have worked with dozens of clients across different regions and segments. More so, we have spoken to thousands of financial institutions over 6 years about their digital wealth strategy and Robo-advisor requirements.

Most of those companies have probably explored several of the strategies offered in this chapter, and some have even explored multiple strategies in parallel. At the end of the day, the fact is that nearly all have ultimately chosen some other strategy than a pure in-house build. They may combine pieces from a platform they bought, license other parts from a Robo-advisor platform, and maintain an in-house team to do the rest. That's perfectly acceptable and increasingly common.

In my experience, the main reason it is hard to build a Robo-advisor is stakeholder paralysis, or conflict between stakeholders. The larger the company, the more stakeholders you will have. For example, start with some simple questions: Which department should own the Robo-advisor? If you don't have a digital wealth team in place, does it belong to IT? Usually not for strategic channels. Perhaps it should be run under the wealth business, or securities, or products. Who runs the requirements gathering? How do you then ensure proper guidance from legal and compliance on regulatory matters? How much control over the requirements and delivery should you grant to IT?

It goes on and on – not just before the project, but especially during the implementation phase. The closer you get to launch, the more obstacles will start popping up as various stakeholder teams want to cover their career capital. The obvious solution to this is to bring in some form of ready-made technology. It opens up a few tricky questions around intellectual property, infrastructure, and security, but unlocks any stakeholder paralysis by resolving flexibility around requirements dictated by whatever platform capabilities come along with the chosen Robo-advisor platform.

All of this mostly applies to financial institutions. There is a genuine use case for building a Robo-advisor, which is when that is your only business.

Building a Robo-advisor start-up

Given that the Robo-advisor industry was started by start-ups, it's only natural that more arrive every year. Unlike something universal such as taxis and food delivery, the nature of financial services makes it hard for one platform to go global and dominate. This leaves a rich landscape of opportunities of every shape and size for local Robo-advisor start-ups to tackle.

When it comes to start-ups, a key decision is around the business model. The obvious distinction will be between go-to-market routes, whether B2C or B2B. Those opting for B2C will need to take care of all the requirements outlined in the previous chapter, beyond the basic algorithms. First and foremost, the specialized staff and extra capital required to seek regulatory licensing are high barriers to entry.

Those seeking glory in the B2B market will need a different kind of expertise in terms of working with clients on digital strategy, complex integrations, and B2B sales. Part of the challenge in B2B will be around platform strategy. While intuitively, the appeal and success of SaaS platforms in other use cases such as payments and lending will make it seem like a no-brainer, it's important to note that Robo-advisory is even more localized than most other fintech categories. Serving small financial advisor groups in America will not translate automatically to doing the same in the UK or Australia, let alone UAE or China. This makes the market for a SaaS offering dangerously narrow, and only appropriate for large domestic markets such as the US. For most B2B Robo-advisors, the only realistic path is some form of COTS solution, often in the form of APIs complemented by customized code depending on client requirements.

It's worth noting that it's perfectly legitimate for a Robo-advisor start-up to leverage other start-up resources. Investors would not expect 100% of code to be in-house, just whatever you consider core intellectual property. Therefore, it helps to take advantage of the rich swathe of API-based providers across capabilities such as custody, brokerage, KYC, AML, chatbots, or even rebalancing.

Well, that covers most of my experience in decision-making around Robo-advisors and whether you should build, buy, or lease.

Summary

In this chapter, we've examined the thought processes involved in deciding whether to build a Robo-advisor. We started by covering the simple case of an individual, and why you might want to learn about the inner workings of a Robo-advisor in addition to, or as an alternative to, simply using an online Robo-advisor. For those already engaging in algorithmic trading, or pursuing a career in digital wealth, it should be well worth the time spent in learning, even if you don't end up managing your money with your own Robo-advisor long term.

For businesses, the question is much more nuanced. We explored separately the concerns around buying, leasing, or building a Robo-advisor. We began by looking at the most common approach, which is leasing or licensing. There, we explored some of the differences in leasing and licensing models, from SaaS to API and COTS-based implementations. Most businesses should find a workable solution from that list, with smaller advisory groups preferring low-cost ones with minimal customization, and large institutions seeking highly customized platforms with big enterprise budgets.

We also looked at the decision-making criteria around buying versus building, and the scenarios in which both could be a solid strategy or a fool's errand. Ultimately, most Robo-advisor start-ups will end up needing to build at least most of their platform themselves as a commitment to proprietary technology and intellectual property. Most other companies may dip their toes into a custom build, but eventually end up with a hybrid combination of building some and leasing the rest.

This chapter also concludes *Part 1* of the book, in which we have set the stage for finally getting our hands dirty. So far, we have built a solid foundation of understanding about Robo-advisors, where they came from, why they became popular, how they work, and how we should approach building one. In the next chapter, we will start with some Python basics before diving into building our first Robo-advisor capabilities one by one.

Part 2: Building Your Own Robo-Advisor

Part 2 of this book is a hands-on guide to building the necessary components of a Robo-advisor, whether for your own personal use or for a business.

This section has the following chapters:

5

Basic Setup and Requirements for Building a Robo-Advisor

This chapter will serve as the gateway into the hands-on coding chapters that form *Part 2* and the rest of this book. The remaining chapters will focus on functional implementations of various Robo-advisor capabilities, so we will dedicate this chapter to setting up the tools required to do so.

However, this will not be a sufficient tutorial for those wholly unfamiliar with Python and coding. While the coding skills required for this book are relatively basic, you may choose to brush up on your Python skills or learn some basics using other online resources. A few good places to start include websites such as `www.Python.org`, `www.LearnPython.org`, or `www.Coursera.org`.

In this chapter, we're going to cover the following topics:

- Installing and setting up Python for the hands-on chapters
- Installing and setting up the required Python modules
- Importing, reading, and visualizing market data

Installing and setting up Python for the hands-on chapters

There are many ways in which you can run Python code, which is what we need to do. For the sake of simplicity and independence from which device you're using, I will recommend Google Colab. The main benefit of using Colab over other popular solutions is that it is free, runs on your browser, and requires no setup whatsoever.

If you have other requirements or preferences, you can explore other popular Python offline installations such as Anaconda. The main benefit of Anaconda is that you can work entirely offline without the need for an internet connection. Anaconda offers both browser-based editing with Jupyter and a dedicated desktop application in Spyder. If that seems more appropriate to your needs, you can go to `https://docs.anaconda.com/anaconda/install/`.

You can also access and download all the code for the chapters in this book's GitHub repo here: `https://github.com/PacktPublishing/Robo-Advisor-with-Python`.

Starting Google Colab

To get started with Colab, just go to `https://colab.research.google.com`. You should see the following welcome page with a brief tutorial and plenty of useful links:

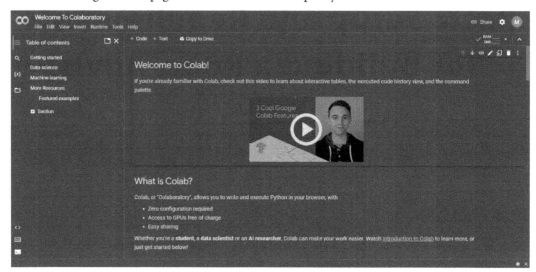

Figure 5.1 – Google Colab welcome screen

Despite its relative simplicity in development tools, there are still a lot of features within Colab that we won't be using. So, don't worry about trying to explore all its capabilities right away – we'll use what we need as we go along.

As it says on the tutorial page, these Colab pages are Jupyter notebooks. If you already have Jupyter notebooks on your computer, you can upload them to Colab. Similarly, if you start on Colab but decide later you prefer to work offline, you can simply install Anaconda and download your Colab worksheets to run on Jupyter instead. You'll find instructions on all this and more on Colab itself.

While not strictly necessary for following this book, I would highly recommend using the **Sign In** feature at the top-right corner before moving forward. So long as you have a Google account of some sort, work or private, you can connect Colab to your Google Drive folders to store all your work for later. Colab will then automatically create a **Colab Notebooks** folder under **My Drive**, which will store all your Colab files going forward. Pretty neat!

In Colab, to run a block of code, you just need to click the play button, which becomes highlighted on the left-hand side of the block if you move your mouse anywhere over a block of code:

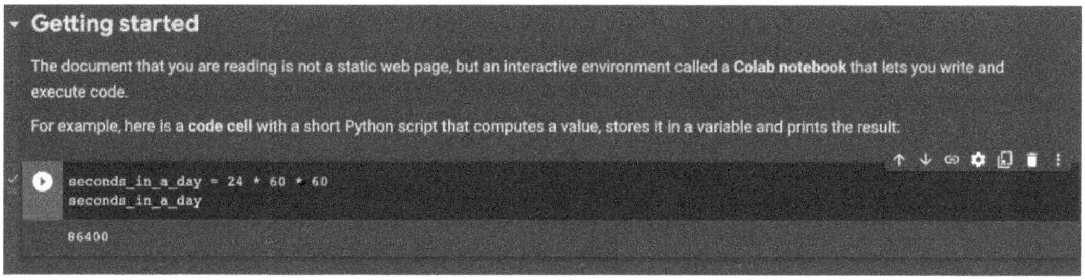

Figure 5.2 – Running code on Colab

The first time you press the play button, it will take a few seconds to connect to Colab's online Python service to run your code. At the top right, instead of **Connect**, you should now see a green checkmark next to the indicators for **RAM** and **Disk**, which refer to available memory and storage, respectively. Once the code has been run, there will be another green checkmark on the left-hand side of your code block, and an indication of the number of seconds needed to run your code.

The beauty of Python on Colab especially is that results are shown just below your code. This allows you to structure notebooks that are structured like documents and can include notes or descriptions between blocks of code, just like on the welcome page itself.

Now that we have the tool we need, let's start making use of it for our Robo-advisor project.

Working with Colab notebooks

The first thing we need to do is start a new notebook by clicking **File** > **New notebook** from the top menu.

Once we have a fresh empty notebook, the first thing we should do is rename the file to something useful. You can use whatever you like, but possibly the most useful might be something referring to the project and/or chapter. If you want a long file that will contain all your code, something like `Roboadvisor.ipynb` could work. Alternatively, by chapter, you could use `Robo-advisor - Chapter 5.ipynb`, which is what I'm opting for. If you're wondering what the strange file format `ipynb` is, then it's the format used by Jupyter for its notebooks, which is what Colab is based on.

If you've signed in with your Google account, as you should, then this new file will be automatically stored on your Google Drive, as follows:

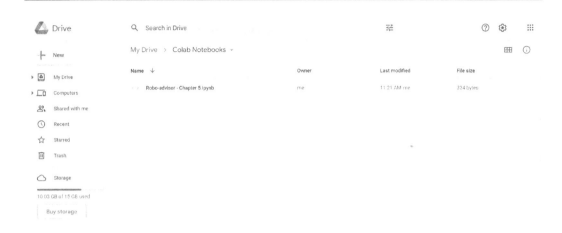

Figure 5.3 – Colab notebooks are stored automatically on your Google Drive

If you close your browser or even use another computer, you can access and continue working on the same notebook directly from your Google Drive by just double-clicking on the file. If you haven't signed in to Colab yet, do so now to avoid losing your work later on.

Changes you make to notebooks are also automatically saved, assuming you have a working internet connection. As mentioned earlier, if you need to work on your project without the internet, then prepare by downloading an offline client using Anaconda and Jupyter (or Spyder). To make your Colab files available offline, just go to **File**, then **Download**, and click on **Download .ipynb**. These files can be opened directly on Jupyter or Spyder.

That covers the bare essentials for us to run some code. Now, we need to add some more specific tools needed for our Robo-advisor project.

Installing and setting up the required Python modules

While there are some parts of our code that we can write using purely primitive Python functions, our work will be made much easier by using Python modules. A module is a piece of code written and published by someone else, that you can use for free. That's the beauty of modern open source software – there are very few limits to productivity and creativity. Modules allow us to build on the shoulders of giants, as it were.

Another benefit of Colab is that it always runs a fresh version of Python and many popular modules, so there is less hassle in downloading, installing, and upgrading these different versions. Trust me, it can become quite a hassle over time when you start getting conflicts between different modules.

We will be making use of several popular modules, including NumPy, SciPy, pandas, and matplotlib, in addition to some more specific to finance that we will install when needed. By way of example, though, I've highlighted the general process here:

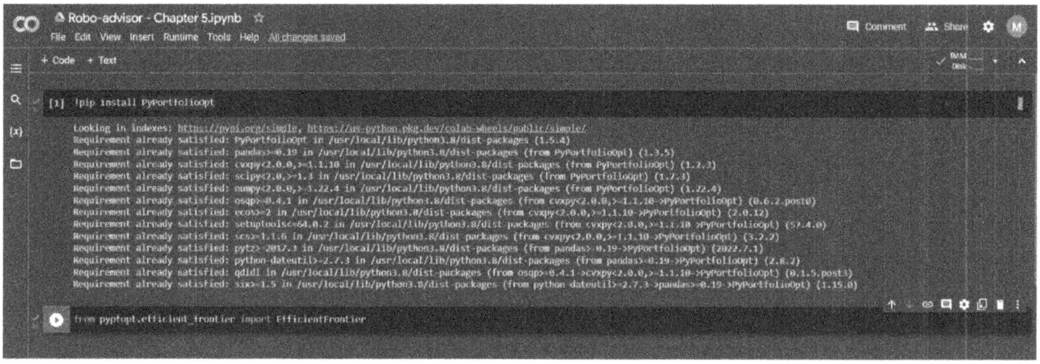

Figure 5.4 – Installing and importing a Python module

Only two steps are needed to install and use any Python module that isn't already available on Colab. To find out whether it is available, you can try an import statement. If you get an error stating "no module named, then you probably need to install it first:

1. Find a module you need to install. If you don't know the name of it, you can often find what you need by googling Python module and whatever keyword or function it is you're after. Most modules have websites or dedicated pages on GitHub, a popular open source code repository. There, you'll typically find instructions for installation, usage, and a complete reference of functions available.

2. Check if the module is already installed:

    ```
    from <module> import <function>
    ```

3. If you get an error, then you need to install the module:

    ```
    !pip install <module>
    ```

4. Retry running the import statement – hopefully, you'll see green checkmarks and no errors, which means you're now able to use the module and its functions.

Don't worry, though – when we need modules that are not available on Colab, I'll be sure to call them out and we'll install them on the spot. Let's do one right now to gain access to some market data.

Importing, reading, and visualizing market data

If you're going to code something relating to finance, chances are you're going to need some market data. In practical terms, what we're after is some price history data on stocks and funds that we'll use to build our portfolios later on. Luckily, there are a few free and easy sources available online. The oldest and most reliable is Yahoo Finance, which has been used by hobbyists and professionals alike for more than a decade.

It is worth noting that the specific modules and functions we will use in this book are subject to change. As each module is an open source project run by volunteers, they are particularly prone to changes in names or being entirely abandoned. If you find that some of the code in this book no longer works, then use Google to find alternative modules or functions – you should find something that works. To minimize this annoyance, I have tried to use well-established and popular modules as much as possible.

So, let's get some market data. We'll start by installing the yfinance module:

1. Simply run the following line of code. We used version 0.2.4:

    ```
    !pip install yfinance
    ```

2. From here, we can call functions using the shorthand yf. Let's try it out:

    ```
    import yfinance as yf
    msft = yf.Ticker("MSFT")
    hist = msft.history(period="max")
    ```

    Now, we have the daily historical prices for Microsoft going back to its IPO date in 1986. Pretty neat! What's even cooler is that we can show it on a graph. Let's do that now.

3. Let's install another module called mplfinance. We used version 0.12.9b7:

    ```
    !pip install mplfinance
    ```

4. Once installed, we must import the module using our abbreviated name, mpf, reuse our Microsoft data, and create a nice line plot using the plot function:

    ```
    import mplfinance as mpf
    mpf.plot(hist,type='line')
    ```

    When you run the code, you should see something like this:

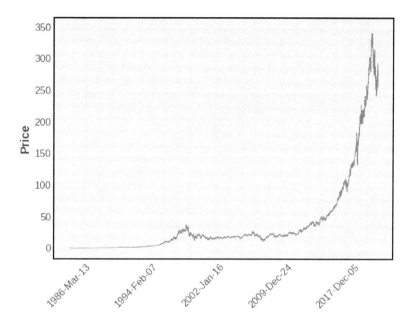

Figure 5.5 – Historical daily prices for Microsoft

Another useful tool we will add to our arsenal is the `DataReader` function from the standard `pandas` module. We won't need to install this, but just import what we need to get easily formatted data on stocks:

```
from pandas_datareader import data as pdr
yf.pdr_override()
data = pdr.get_data_yahoo("SPY", start="2017-01-01",
    end="2017-04-30")
mpf.plot(data,type='line')
```

This gets us a snapshot of daily closing prices for the popular S&P 500 ETF, which is used as a universal benchmark for financial markets. We can now visualize this second dataset like we did the first, to see what we got:

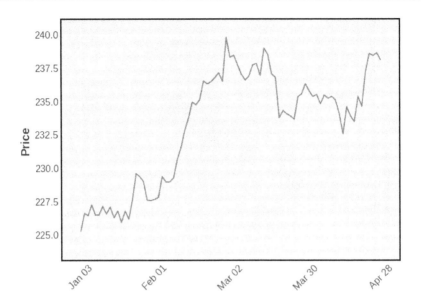

Figure 5.6 – Price history for the popular SPY ETF

How easy was that? Now, you see how much easier our lives are made by using open source modules and running on Colab. This minimizes our time fiddling around with esoteric programming and computer compatibility issues, which can take up an enormous portion of a professional developer's time and energy.

Going forward, depending on our needs, we will use other additional modules and functions to manipulate and format market data to our specific needs.

Summary

This chapter has given us the basic tools we will need to build our Robo-advisor. We started by choosing Colab as our Python development tool. Those who prefer to work offline could opt to install the popular Anaconda Python environment on their local machine and use browser (Jupyter) or desktop (Spyder) applications as their editors. At the end of the day, all will work, but to get started quickly and easily, Colab is the way to go.

Once we established some file management tools available on Colab, we created our first notebook. As a reminder, should you choose to switch to offline later, you can download your Colab notebooks and run them on Jupyter or Spyder.

With our first notebook, we tried installing additional modules that were not already included in Colab and downloaded some samples of market data. We will be using market data from Yahoo Finance extensively in this book to implement and test our Robo-advisor capabilities as we go along. Finally, we used another module to create simple visualizations of our market data, which will be another useful tool to carry with us.

With that, we have what we need to start building our first Robo-advisor capabilities in earnest. The rest of this book will proceed logically using the workflow we established in *Chapter 2, What Makes Up a Robo-Advisor?*

6
Goal-Based Investing

This chapter begins our journey toward building a Robo-advisor hands-on. We will begin by creating some basic objects that we will need along the way, and exploring some useful Python methods that will make our life easier as we build up our capabilities. Throughout the book, our framework for investing will be Goal-based investing, so this chapter will form the basis of many other features that use the concept of Goals in different ways.

Before we jump into some code, let's briefly talk about why Goals are important. You might be tempted to skip past Goals altogether and just build a portfolio of **Exchange-Traded Funds** (**ETFs**). Let me try and convince you otherwise. One of the core challenges of investing, in general, is psychology. In one sense, the idea is simple. Invest as much as you can, and buy and hold like Warren Buffet. In reality, life and investing are much more complicated. The simplicity of a single portfolio and a single risk profile simply does not work in the long term for most people.

The benefit of Goals is three-fold. Firstly, each investment now has a specific set of reasons for it. It's no longer just money – it's your first home, your dream car, your retirement on a sailboat. Whatever it is you want in life, you're thinking of it specifically as something to save and invest toward with a specific time horizon in mind. Now, your investment has a reason, a date, an amount, and maybe even a photo. This type of personalization will also motivate you toward additional savings. Accelerating your investment portfolio accumulation is great and all, but accelerating moving into your dream home is a lot more tangible.

That makes it much easier to then consider risk in the context of your Goal, the second benefit. Your attitude toward money and markets will change regularly, but it's easier to think of it in terms of a specific Goal. For example, if markets go against you, are you okay to delay retirement or alter your retirement lifestyle? If yes, then by how much? You might be more flexible with retirement, but what about your child's college fund? If the returns fall short of expectations, will you ask little Timmy to take a gap year? These parameters will tell you how much risk you can actually afford in the context of your Goal.

There is a third consideration around portfolios and accounts, and mapping those to your Goal(s). This will obviously depend tremendously on your custodian and what reporting they can offer. Generally, being able to report performance at the Goal level will be another way to increase your commitment to your Goals. Having the ability to choose risk levels per Goal will enable users to separate low-risk Goals from high-risk Goals, instead of lumping everything into an average, moderate portfolio.

I hope that gives you further motivation to stick with Goals as the basis of our Robo-advisor. If you do not wish to use Goals, you can simply skip this chapter. If you do wish to use Goals, let's go right ahead!

In this chapter, we're going to cover the following topics:

- Creating your first investment Goal using Python
- Modeling and creating different types of investment Goals
- Creating necessary objects for investment Goals
- Learning different approaches to tying Goals to accounts

Creating your first investment Goal using Python

Let's pick things up from where we left off in the previous chapter. Open up Google Colab in your browser of choice, and either continue in your existing Colab notebook or create a new one for this chapter.

If you don't have much experience with programming languages, then a key concept you will need to learn about is **classes**. To make it simple, a class is a place to store information that you want to reuse in your code. This helps avoid having to write the same code over and over again, which is a common source of errors. Goals are something we plan to reuse across our code, and therefore it's useful to define some details about Goals to make our life easier later on. This prevents us from having to copy and paste sections of code including lists of variables and will help us maintain code that can be easily updated when changes are needed.

In our situation, the first useful class will be `Goal`. This is because we will use and reference various details about Goals throughout our code later on. By creating a class for Goals, we can simply use the `Goal` class whenever we need Goal features. If we need different details later on, we just need to update one piece of code in our `Goal` class.

Let's try this in practice. Let's think about what details might be useful for a Goal:

```
goalName = "Retirement"
goalTarget = 3000000
```

For exploring some concepts, this is fine; but it will quickly become problematic. Imagine we need to keep adding more details about Goals. It means, we will have to remember the name of the variables that we defined, where we used them, and keep copy-pasting the code back and forth to keep everything running. This becomes especially cumbersome if we need to keep lists of these details for several Goals.

Instead, we can just define a class called `Goal`:

```
class Goal:
  def __init__(self, name, target):
```

```
self.name = name
self.target= target
```

Remember that in Google Colab, you need to execute your code by clicking the play button next to your code block. To follow along with this book and our code examples, it's usually helpful to create new code blocks for every new piece of code. That will help you test and organize your code for later reference.

Generally, Python is a very friendly and easy language, with little extra code needed to make things work. However, you still need to learn some grammar, or syntax, to understand how to make Python do what you need to accomplish. One of those details is the __init__ constructor **function** highlighted in the preceding code. The job of this function is to define two things: what details we wish to store about our class, and how those details get stored.

In Python, those details are called **properties**. In the preceding code, name and target are the properties I've chosen for our Goal class. The self keyword is a reference to the class itself. So what we're doing is saying that a Goal has these two properties. Now we can create our first Goal!

```
class Goal:
    def __init__(self, name, target):
        self.name = name
        self.target= target

                         (name, target) -> None
    myGoal = Goal(())
```

Figure 6.1 – Hovering hint for our Goal class

One of the incredibly helpful features of Google Colab is that it will remember the classes and functions we create. As soon as you start typing a statement that contains our new class, you will see an automatic hint appear over our code that reminds us which properties we need to create a new Goal:

```
myGoal = Goal("Retirement", 3000000)
```

Once you execute this code block, you've created your first Goal. We can now use the myGoal variable whenever we need to use this particular Goal. We can obviously create as many Goals as we need by using other variable names. Remember, a class is just a recipe. That recipe only creates a dish when you use it. In coding, that means calling the class constructor function and assigning the result to a variable, which is what we've just done.

Let's see what we can do with this new Goal:

```
print(myGoal.name)
print(myGoal.target)
```

The output will be the following:

```
Retirement
3000000
```

As you can see, our `Goal` class is useful storage of any information we may want to keep about our Goals. We can also change them later on if we need to:

```
myGoal.target = 1000000
print(myGoal.target)
```

The output will be as follows:

```
1000000
```

Now that we have our basic Goal available to use, we will look at a wider definition of the Goals that will be required for a Robo-advisor.

Modeling and creating different types of investment Goals

Typically, the most important Goal for any Robo-advisor is a retirement Goal. This applies to countries where social security isn't prevalent or sufficient to support life beyond full-time employment as we enter our golden years. So, let's begin by thinking about how we might model a retirement Goal using Python.

Before we write any more code, we should step back to consider what information would be necessary to create a Goal for retirement. The first thing that comes to mind is time. In most countries, the retirement age is defined by law, although it keeps being pushed back now and then. Nevertheless, we would assume that whatever money we need for retirement should be made available on the date of our retirement. That means we need to know our current age, to know how much time there is between now and retirement.

Another useful thing might be the ability to give a name to our Goal. Research shows that naming things increases commitment. Given that retirement is expensive, we should also consider how we will be saving up—both in terms of existing savings and our ability to add savings each month. Let's put this all together.

While we could add these directly to our `Goal` class, it would be premature. Only some of these apply to all other types of Goals. Imagine we're saving for a boat. It's hardly relevant to ask what retirement age is required for our boat. So, let's start by adding the properties we believe to be universal across all imaginable Goals we might want to use in our Robo-advisor. Don't worry, thanks to our `Goal` class, we can always change these if we change our minds or think of new properties. Following is the code for what our current `Goal` class will look like:

```python
class Goal:
    def __init__(self, name, targetYear, targetValue,
        initialContribution=0, monthlyContribution=0):
        self.name = name
        self.targetYear = targetYear
        self.targetValue = targetValue
        self.initialContribution = initialContribution
        self.monthlyContribution = monthlyContribution
```

Another useful tip for Python classes is that we can mark some properties as optional. This allows us to create a new Goal without necessarily knowing all the details needed for all properties. They can then be added at a later time:

```python
myGoal = Goal("Retirement", 2060, 3000000)
myGoal.initialContribution = 10000
```

What about retirement age? Well, we could do one of two things. We could calculate that year separately and use the `targetYear` property to store it as shown here:

```python
from datetime import date
retirementAge = 65
startingAge = 41
targetYear = date.today().year + (retirementAge-startingAge)
myGoal.targetYear = targetYear
print(myGoal.targetYear)
```

This will give you the right answer. But if this is something you need to create routinely, we might as well create something reusable. In Python, that takes the form of inheriting a class. **Inheritance** just means we want to keep all the good ideas we had with our `Goal` class, but add some new properties that only apply to certain types of Goals:

```python
class RetirementGoal(Goal):
    def __init__(self, name, targetValue, startingAge,
        retirementAge):
```

```
        targetYear = date.today().year + (
            retirementAge-startingAge)
        super().__init__(name, targetYear, targetValue)
        self.retirementAge = retirementAge
```

To reuse our `Goal` class, we simply include it in the definition line of our new class called `RetirementGoal`. To make sure we store the required properties that we defined in our `Goal` class, we call the `super()` function, which, in this case, calls the `__init__` function inside the `Goal` class. This helps us avoid duplicating definitions for the previously defined properties, and gives us the flexibility to calculate those property values on the fly as we did with `targetYear`. The new property for retirement age will not be included in `Goal` and is only specific to `RetirementGoal`. Let's try this inherited class in action:

```
myRetirement = RetirementGoal("Honolulu", 3000000, 41, 60)
print(myRetirement.targetYear)
```

This shows you how handy it was to move our little calculation for the target year inside the new class, which is specific to retirement. This is a trick that can be used extensively as we build complexity into our Robo-advisor.

Let's look at some other potential examples of Goal types that could be useful:

```
class GrowWealthGoal(Goal):
    def __init__(self, initialContribution, monthlyContribution):
        targetYear = date.today().year + 10
        targetAmount = 1000000
        super().__init__("Grow My Wealth", targetYear,
        targetAmount, initialContribution, monthlyContribution)
```

Actually, one of the more popular Goals on most Robo-advisors is a generic investment Goal, typically named something such as **Grow My Wealth**. After all, this is a catch-all bucket for when you don't yet have something specific in mind. This implementation is just one way of doing it, assuming the investor has no specific time horizon or amount in mind. In which case, you could just ask them how much savings and spare income they can funnel into this Goal and set an arbitrary time horizon of 10 years and 1 million dollars. Again, this is just an example showing how different questions are relevant to different types of Goals.

Another very popular Goal is education, which typically means saving for your children's college fund. Let's look at an example implementation here:

```
class EducationGoal(Goal):
    def __init__(self, name, startYear, degreeLengthYears,
      annualTuitionFees, degreeType, schoolName):
```

```
    targetValue = degreeLengthYears * annualTuitionFees
    super().__init__(name, startYear, targetValue)
    self.degreeType = degreeType
    self.schoolName = schoolName
```

We're still using the same Goal class as our underlying object, but now we need to convert education-specific properties into a target value for our investment. In this case, that would be the product of duration of degree and the annual tuition fees. Certainly, there might be more elaborate versions of EducationGoal imaginable.

To round out our trio of core investment Goals, let's add a home Goal:

```
class RealEstateGoal(Goal):
    def __init__(self, name, targetYear, homeValue, downPayment,
      mortgagePayment, interestRate):
      targetValue = downPayment
      super().__init__(name, targetYear, targetValue)
      self.homeValue = homeValue
      self.downPayment = downPayment
      self.mortgagePayment = mortgagePayment
      self.interestRate = interestRate
```

What makes a real-estate Goal different from those before is that we're not actually saving the whole amount of homeValue. That would take too long. Instead, we only save and invest toward the down payment amount, which we pass to the Goal class constructor.

Finally, here's something that you don't see as much on current Robo-advisors but could be a fun addition to capture the current zeitgeist. How about a Goal for your own start-up?

```
class StartupGoal(Goal):
    def __init__(self, companyName, startYear, seedFunding):
      super().__init__(companyName, startYear, seedFunding)
```

This example also shows that there might be reasons to create a child class even in cases where we have no special properties in mind. If nothing else, it lets us set the input parameters to be relevant to the start-up theme, and the optionality to add other properties such as a company logo later on. Such a Goal would allow you to save and invest in your own seed funding, rather than having to rely on raising external capital to get started.

These were all examples of long-term plans that have a key pre-requisite for investing: enough time for compound interest to work its magic. Remember: with risk comes volatility; so something you plan to do next summer isn't a good idea for an investment Goal. Besides not making a return, there is a significant chance your money would actually lose value during that period. While that is always possible for any time horizon, the longer you wait, the lower that statistical probability remains.

So, what should you do about short-term savings, then? Well, we could create a separate cash-only type of Goal with no investment or portfolio:

```
class SavingsGoal:
  def __init__(self, name, targetDate, targetValue,
    initialContribution, monthlyContribution):
    self.name = name
    self.targetDate = targetDate
    self.targetValue = targetValue
    self.initialContribution = initialContribution
    self.monthlyContribution = monthlyContribution
```

The key difference here is that we've set the cash contribution amounts as mandatory. After all, if we're not investing and the time horizon is a specific date, we need to make sure we're putting aside enough cash here. We can do that by adding some additional code that calculates how much savings will be accumulated with the parameters provided:

```
class SavingsGoal:
  def __init__(self, name, targetDate, targetValue,
    initialContribution, monthlyContribution):
    from dateutil import parser
    targetDateTime = parser.parse(targetDate)
    from dateutil.relativedelta import relativedelta
    delta = relativedelta(targetDateTime, date.today())
    difference_in_months = delta.months + delta.years * 12
    value = initialContribution + (monthlyContribution *
        difference_in_months)
    print(value)
    if not (value >= targetValue):
            raise ValueError('Target value too high to be
            achieved.')
    self.name = name
    self.targetDate = targetDateTime
    self.targetValue = targetValue
    self.initialContribution = initialContribution
    self.monthlyContribution = monthlyContribution
```

This time, you'll notice this is no longer a child class of Goal. The main reason is that we don't intend to invest in these Goals, so we won't be linking this type of Goal to a portfolio later on. This SavingsGoal class is therefore entirely independent of our previous definitions. Of course, you could go ahead and define a structure with a more generic Goal class, and then add child classes for InvestmentGoal and SavingsGoal. Whatever works for you.

In the previous example, the interesting feature we've added is an error in case SavingsGoal doesn't make sense. We use a bit of Python magic to extract the date and calculate how many months are left before the Goal is due. If the math doesn't add up for you to meet your target amount by that deadline, then we show an error. Let's see this in practice:

```
from dateutil.relativedelta import relativedelta
new_date = date.today() + relativedelta(years=1)
new_date = new_date.strftime("%B %d, %Y")
saver = SavingsGoal("Rainy Day", new_date, 10000, 1000, 100)
```

Once you run that line of code, which just adds exactly 1 year to today's date, you'll see something like this:

```
 2200
-------------------------------------------------------------
ValueError                         Traceback (most recent call last)
Cell In[24], line 1
----> 1 saver = SavingsGoal("Rainy Day", new_date, 10000, 1000,
100)

Cell In[12], line 11, in SavingsGoal.__init__(self,
name, targetDate, targetValue, initialContribution,
monthlyContribution)
      9 print(value)
     10 if not (value >= targetValue):
---> 11          raise ValueError('Target value too high to be
achieved.')
     12 self.name = name
     13 self.targetDate = targetDateTime

ValueError: Target value too high to be achieved.
```

What we can see is that it works. Our convenient `print` statement shows us that the best we can do in this timeframe is $2,200, well short of our $10,000 target. So let's try something different:

```
saver = SavingsGoal("Rainy Day", new_date, 10000, 1000, 1000)
```

This should print out $13,000 with no errors:

13000

Success! Now let's imagine some further Goals that would be worth saving for:

```
class WeddingGoal(SavingsGoal):
    def __init__(self, name, weddingDate, budget,
      initialContribution, monthlyContribution):
        super().__init__(name, weddingDate, budget,
          initialContribution, monthlyContribution)
        self.weddingDate = weddingDate


class TravelGoal(SavingsGoal):
    def __init__(self, destination, tripDate, tripDuration,
      budget, initialContribution, monthlyContribution):
        super().__init__(destination, tripDate, budget,
          initialContribution, monthlyContribution)
        self.tripDuration = tripDuration


class SplurgeGoal(SavingsGoal):
    def __init__(self, itemName, storeName, targetPurchaseDate,
      budget, initialContribution, monthlyContribution):
        super().__init__(itemName + " @ " + storeName,
          targetPurchaseDate, budget, initialContribution,
          monthlyContribution)
```

Weddings, holiday travel, and big purchases all fall under the category of Goals that have very specific budgets and dates. Maybe you want to save up for a Christmas gift budget. There is zero flexibility in that schedule, even less so for a wedding. That means you can ill afford the volatility of investing, so it's best to put away cold hard cash instead.

Let's test out `SplurgeGoal`, which has another little feature of using the item and store names together for the Goal name:

```
new_date = date.today() + relativedelta(months=3)
new_date = new_date.strftime("%B %d, %Y")
```

```
goal = SplurgeGoal("MacBook", "Apple", new_date, 1500, 500,
    500)
goal.name
```

This would print out "MacBook @ Apple".

Let's take a look at one last type of Goal that could be relevant to our project. Thus far, we've focused on accumulation, which is simply adding money. This is certainly relevant for most cases, but there is also a scenario in which you have already saved a certain amount and simply wish to have it last for a given period. This is called decumulation. Let's reimagine our earlier RetirementGoal class now as a decumulation version:

```
class IncomeGoal:
  def __init__(self, durationYears, startingValue,
    monthlyDividend):
    self.durationYears = durationYears
    self.startingValue = startingValue
    self.monthlyDividend = monthlyDividend


class RetirementIncome(IncomeGoal):
  def __init__(self, retirementSavings, currentAge,
    retirementAge, retirementIncome):
    lifeExpectancy = 79
    durationYears = lifeExpectancy - retirementAge
    super().__init__(durationYears, retirementSavings,
        retirementIncome)
    self.retirementYear = date.today().year + (
        retirementAge-currentAge)
```

Given the different focus, we've omitted using the Goal class as our parent class to start from scratch. As our key properties, we're now interested in paying ourselves from our savings. In reality, this could take many forms depending on which type of investment products are at your disposal. For something such as a retirement income Goal, one could imagine still investing your nest egg in a conservative portfolio with a high dividend yield. The modest growth target of the portfolio will help sustain the monthly income for a longer period than a straight draw-down.

This has by no means been a conclusive or exhaustive exploration of what is possible with Goals, but it gives you plenty to work with for your Robo-advisor project. Now let's look at some supplementary code that will help us work with our Goals going forward.

Creating necessary objects for investment Goals

What if you don't know how much you need for retirement or a wedding? Well, for starters, you could use Google. Of course, depending on where you live or where you plan to retire, some of the information you find could be quite misleading. Then, you'd have to make some assumptions about inflation for Goals that are decades into the future. Quickly, this can become overwhelming in complexity for the average investor. Let's look at one possible approach to assist. In the following screenshot, we're looking at an example of using a questionnaire to gather retirement Goal inputs.

Figure 6.2 – Example from Bambu's Goal Helper API

From the screenshot, you'll see several complementary methods of estimating Goals. Let's break them down:

- We use proxy questions to estimate the target Goal amount when the target amount itself isn't simple to decide. If you want to buy a car, you can just look up the price. For retirement, it is mainly driven by lifestyle costs. In the Bambu implementation, investors can choose a cost level between **Basic** and **Luxurious** across six cost categories: housing, transport, healthcare, food, recreation, and miscellaneous. Each category has an underlying dataset of national or state-level price indices to come up with a number. For example, retirement in South Dakota is naturally cheaper than in New York or California. A similar approach works equally well for things such as real estate, where it is even possible to look up real-time prices for a given area.

- To further assist investors in picking the right cost levels, we can pre-empt by prefilling levels appropriate to their current income level. This can be baselined by income deciles, again on a national or state level.

- Inflation-based compounding can be applied automatically to prices to ensure we aren't artificially aiming too low.

- The output will be a monthly cost of living in retirement, adjusted for inflation. Further assumptions about retirement age and life expectancy are required to come up with a lump sum target amount. This lump sum will serve as a basis for decumulation, either on a cash or partially invested basis, as discussed previously in this chapter.

Building something like this is beyond the scope of this book, but for those keen to offer such capabilities, you could simply use Bambu's API Library (`https://developer.bambu.co/`) to add Goal helpers to your Robo-advisor platform. Bambu provides such Goal helpers for many popular Goals such as retirement, education, and home.

Another important question to ask yourself about your Goal is how important is it to you at this time? This is particularly relevant when you are planning for multiple Goals all competing for the same savings to feed them. There are several frameworks defined for this purpose, but here is one proposed by Brunel (Brunel). His Goal Probability Table gives us a simple way to decide the relative importance of Goals.

Realize	Avoid	MinP	MaxP
Dreams	Concerns	0.5	0.64
Wishes	Worries	0.65	0.79
Wants	Fears	0.8	0.89
Needs	Nightmares	0.9	0.99

Figure 6.3 – Brunel's Goal Probability Table

This table can be used to choose an appropriate category based on both positive aspirations as well as negative fears we wish to avoid. It also introduces the associated property of Goal probability, which we will dive into in depth in time. Meanwhile, we could simply add another property to our `Goal` class to reflect this choice:

```
class Goal:
  def __init__(self, name, targetYear, targetValue,
    initialContribution=0, monthlyContribution=0, priority=""):
    self.name = name
    self.targetYear = targetYear
    self.targetValue = targetValue
    self.initialContribution = initialContribution
    self.monthlyContribution = monthlyContribution
    if not (priority == "") and not (priority in ["Dreams",
        "Wishes", "Wants", "Needs"]):
            raise ValueError('Wrong value set for Priority')
    self.priority = priority
```

To ensure that we only set something from Brunel's choices, we can add another error in case the user tries something funny. This simple addition of a Goal priority property can be useful as we build up our capabilities in later chapters. Now, if we wish to go a bit further, we can implement Brunel's table in our code by importing a CSV corresponding to *Figure 6.2*:

```
def getGoalProbabilities(priority):
  import pandas as pd
  lookupTable=pd.read_csv('/content/drive/MyDrive/Books/Robo-
advisor with Python/Data/Goal Probability Table.csv')
  match = (lookupTable['Realize'] == priority)
  minProb = lookupTable['MinP'][(match)]
  maxProb = lookupTable['MaxP'][(match)]
  return minProb.values[0], maxProb.values[0]
```

This method will find and import the CSV file from Google Drive. Alternatively, you could just upload your files directly in Colab to the `sample_data` folder and replace the path. This method will now return the minimum and maximum probabilities for our chosen Goal priority:

```
myGoal = Goal("Vacation", 2027, 10000, priority="Dreams")
minP, maxP = getGoalProbabilities(myGoal.priority)
print(minP)
print(maxP)
```

The result should be 0.5 and 0.64 in your console. While we're at it, we might as well put these pieces together and start adding class methods to our very important Goal class:

```
class Goal:
  def __init__(self, name, targetYear, targetValue,
    initialContribution=0, monthlyContribution=0, priority=""):
    self.name = name
    self.targetYear = targetYear
    self.targetValue = targetValue
    self.initialContribution = initialContribution
    self.monthlyContribution = monthlyContribution
    if not (priority == "") and not (priority in ["Dreams",
    "Wishes", "Wants", "Needs"]):
        raise ValueError('Wrong value set for Priority.')
    self.priority = priority


  def getGoalProbabilities(self):
    if (self.priority == ""):
        raise ValueError('No value set for Priority.')
    import pandas as pd
    lookupTable=pd.read_csv('/content/drive/MyDrive/Books/Robo-
advisor with Python /Data/Goal Probability Table.csv')
    match = (lookupTable['Realize'] == self.priority)
    minProb = lookupTable['MinP'][(match)]
    maxProb = lookupTable['MaxP'][(match)]
    return minProb.values[0], maxProb.values[0]
```

Here, we want to make sure there is a value set for priority first. Now we can try the example from before but with no need to pass the priority value between methods at all, since it is already stored in Goal:

```
myGoal = Goal("Vacation", 2027, 10000, priority="Dreams")
minP, maxP = myGoal.getGoalProbabilities()
print(minP)
print(maxP)
```

You should see the same result as before. This is also a useful example of how we can add increasing layers of complexity to our classes without burdening our code with various separate pieces of code. Remember that, if you now wish to reuse some of the classes derived from the Goal parent class, you may need to run that code again to ensure the reference to the updated parent class is valid. Similarly, for some of the classes we defined as independent of `Goal`, you may wish to change that relationship or duplicate the method inside those classes.

For now, this is all that we need to manage Goals. We will expand on the concept of Goal probability in *Chapter 9*, *Investment Projections*. To wrap up this exploration, let's touch on some variations we might need to tie our Goals to other core Robo-advisor objects such as portfolios and accounts.

Learning different approaches to tying Goals to accounts

The last thing we need to consider for setting up Goal-based investing for our Robo-advisor is how to map our Goals to other core objects. In the next few chapters, we will introduce four new objects that all have a relationship to Goals: **Risk Profiles**, **Portfolios**, **Performance**, and **Accounts**.

Ideally, to achieve the full intention and power of Goal-based investing, we would want to form the following relationships:

- You should be free to create as many Goals as you wish. This seems fairly obvious, as most people have several financial Goals already, and may wish to add more in the future. Therefore, limiting investors to just one Goal would greatly decrease the capability of our Robo-advisor to assist investors in their holistic financial planning.

- You should be able to define a risk profile separately for each Goal. This is quite crucial because one of the main problems of traditional risk profiling is that one score does not capture your attitude toward money and risk in every imaginable scenario. Being able to answer a risk questionnaire per Goal allows the investor to consider the questions in light of a specific time horizon and scenario. Investors may well be aggressive toward far-away Goals with low priority and highly risk-averse to high-priority Goals in the near future.

> **Note**
> One alternative approach is to use a global risk profile score as a basis for designing Goal-specific portfolios that allow investors to take greater risks in certain scenarios.

- You should be able to build a separate portfolio for each Goal. This seems the cleanest approach, but it's not without its challenges. While it might be possible to build some type of franken-portfolio that takes into account varying levels of risk across multiple time horizons, it just seems an unnecessary complication. When we link risk profiles to model portfolios, we can logically assign risk profiles to Goals to end up with potentially different portfolios for each Goal.

- You should be able to manage multiple Goals under a single account. This one becomes highly specific to your custodian. Differences in fee structure and integration capabilities will define the best approach. Generally, having more than 2-3 accounts would be considered inefficient for fees and reporting purposes. Depending on the custodian, options such as sub or virtual accounts could be an option. When we manage multiple Goals with different portfolios under a single account, the main reporting object becomes the Goal. If the custodian only sees a single account, it is up to the Robo-advisor to separate and calculate performance on a Goal level.

  However, it is very important to note that this approach may not be suitable or even possible in all circumstances. Besides local regulations, limitations may be imposed by local tax laws, custodian fee structures, or even the technical ability of your broker and custodian to track Goals during transactions.

This decision is something you may need to revisit later on in the book, depending on your choices and available partners. That concludes our first hands-on work and has given us our first Robo-advisor capabilities around Goals.

Summary

This chapter gave us the basic tools needed to create and manipulate Goals, a key concept and class for our Goal-based Robo-advisor. We started by creating our very first Goal using basic Python classes, giving us a way to reuse code whenever we need Goals.

We then expanded on the basic concept of a Goal to add various useful properties and child classes for various types of Goals, including retirement, education, and real estate. We added further ideas for savings Goals and income Goals, which might be useful for certain types of investors.

We rounded out our chapter on Goals by exploring potential add-on capabilities such as Goal helpers and Goal priority to further assist investors in their financial planning. Finally, we considered different ways we might need to tie our Goals to other core Robo-advisor objects that we will define in the coming chapters.

Now, let's proceed to add one of those objects in risk profiles and scores.

Further reading

You might be interested in reading some extra information related to the topics discussed in this chapter. Here is a link to an external resource:

- Brunel, Jean L. P. *Goals-Based Wealth Management: An Integrated and Practical Approach to Changing the Structure of Wealth Advisory Practices.* Wiley, 2015.

Risk Profiling and Scoring

In this chapter, we will look at ways to quantify risk for investments and how to score risk appetite for investors. Once we establish some key concepts such as risk tolerance and risk capacity, we will look at examples of potential **risk questionnaires** and put them all together to calculate a risk score. These form the basic mechanisms for investor protection to ensure any investments made are suitable for the investor. The risk score is what we will ultimately use to determine which investments are appropriate, which is calculated based on inputs provided by the investor in the risk questionnaire. This chapter will tie in with the following two chapters that will ultimately allow an investor to decide on an investment plan.

In this chapter, we will cover the following topics:

- Key concepts in risk profiling and scoring
- Creating and answering a risk questionnaire
- Calculating a risk score

Key concepts in risk profiling and scoring

Following from what we established in *Chapter 2, What Makes Up a Robo-Advisor?*, the fundamental basis of Robo-advisors is Markowitz's **Modern Portfolio Theory** (**MPT**). This isn't to say that it is impossible to avoid MPT, but that in most countries, the regulations set by the government for oversight of financial services dictate the usage of at least certain aspects and assumptions of MPT.

One of those assumptions is that investors should only take more risk in return for more rewards or higher returns. This means we need a way to gauge how much variance and volatility the investors are willing to endure in order to achieve a desired investment return. One such approach would be simply asking that exact question in numerical terms, but in reality, that isn't viable for most investors to answer rationally. Therefore, the industry practice has defined proxies for risk in the form of risk tolerance and risk capacity. These can be used separately or together to form what is known as a risk score.

Let's revisit the definitions for these terms:

- **Risk tolerance**: This is a direct, quantifiable measure of how much financial risk an investor is willing to accept, typically calculated on the basis of a standardized questionnaire.

- **Risk capacity**: This is an indirect quantifiable measure of how much financial risk an investor could take without becoming reckless, typically calculated from other metrics such as age, income, and previous investment experience.

- **Risk score**: This is an often proprietary algorithm to combine outputs of risk tolerance and risk capacity, standardized to a range such as 1–5, 1–10, or 1–100.

Later in this chapter, we will use all three elements in practice. Ultimately, what we will need to make informed choices about our portfolio in *Chapter 8, Model Portfolio Construction*, is the risk score. For now, let's start with a risk questionnaire to find values for risk tolerance and risk capacity.

Creating and answering a risk questionnaire

Let's begin by creating a few useful objects that we can use to structure a questionnaire. This will be a simple static example. In reality, you may choose to store your questions in a spreadsheet, database, or file instead:

```python
class RiskQuestion:
  def __init__(self, questionText, weight=1):
    self.questionText = questionText
    self.weight = weight
    self.answers = []


class RiskQuestionAnswer:
  def __init__(self, answerText, score, selected=False):
    self.answerText = answerText
    self.score = score
    self.selected = selected


class RiskQuestionnaire:
  def __init__(self):
    self.questions = []
```

These three classes that we've just defined work together to produce what we need. The `RiskQuestion` class includes a list of answers for risk questions, which we will use to store objects from the `RiskQuestionAnswer` class. There we will include a simple Boolean value to indicate whether an answer has been selected. Finally, we can store our `RiskQuestion` objects inside a list within the `RiskQuestionnaire` class.

Now, let's try to use these new classes in an example. I've used questions from a well-known paper on risk questions by two university personal financial planning professors, *Dr. Ruth Lytton* at Virginia Tech and *Dr. John Grable* at the University of Georgia (Grable Lytton 1999). You can try a full version online at `https://pfp.missouri.edu/research/investment-risk-tolerance-assessment/`.

> **Important note**
>
> At this point in the book, it is important to remind you that this book is not investment advice, nor is any such advice intended in any of its content. If you choose to make investments on the basis of this book, it is your responsibility alone. Similarly, if you choose to use any contents of this book as part of your Robo-advisor, you alone will be responsible for any investment outcomes and/or regulatory compliance.

First, let's create an example of a risk tolerance questionnaire:

```
toleranceQuestionnaire = RiskQuestionnaire()

question1 = RiskQuestion("In general, how would your best
friend describe you as a risk taker?", 2)
question1.answers.append(RiskQuestionAnswer("A real
gambler",4))
question1.answers.append(RiskQuestionAnswer("Willing to take
risks after completing adequate research",3))
question1.answers.append(RiskQuestionAnswer("Cautious",2))
question1.answers.append(RiskQuestionAnswer("A real risk
avoider",1))

question2 = RiskQuestion("You are on a TV game show and can
choose one of the following. Which would you take?")
question2.answers.append(RiskQuestionAnswer("$1,000 in
cash",1))
question2.answers.append(RiskQuestionAnswer("A 50% chance at
winning $5,000",2))
question2.answers.append(RiskQuestionAnswer("A 25% chance at
winning $10,000",3))
question2.answers.append(RiskQuestionAnswer("A 5% chance at
winning $100,000",4))

question3 = RiskQuestion("When you think of the word risk which
of the following words comes to mind first?")
```

```
question3.answers.append(RiskQuestionAnswer("Loss",1))
question3.answers.append(RiskQuestionAnswer("Uncertainty",2))
question3.answers.append(RiskQuestionAnswer("Opportunity",3))
question3.answers.append(RiskQuestionAnswer("Thrill",4))


toleranceQuestionnaire.questions.append(question1)
toleranceQuestionnaire.questions.append(question2)
toleranceQuestionnaire.questions.append(question3)
```

The preceding code yields us a `toleranceQuestionnaire` object of the `RiskQuestionnaire` class, which is populated with three questions and answers with associated weights.

Now, if we wanted to add a further questionnaire for risk capacity, we would need quantified questions about the investor's financial situation and knowledge. These could be simply added as further questions as part of a single questionnaire, separately as a dedicated questionnaire, or even calculated automatically from previous information about the investor and their Goals.

For illustrative purposes, let's create a separate questionnaire for risk capacity. I've put together a few examples of risk capacity questions that I found online from **RBC Global Asset Management (RBC GAM)**:

```
capacityQuestionnaire = RiskQuestionnaire()


question4 = RiskQuestion("You are able to save money
regularly.")
question4.answers.append(RiskQuestionAnswer("Completely
false",1))
question4.answers.append(RiskQuestionAnswer("Somewhat true",2))
question4.answers.append(RiskQuestionAnswer("Completely
true",3))


question5 = RiskQuestion("You can pay all your monthly bills on
time -- including any credit card or other debt.")
question5.answers.append(RiskQuestionAnswer("Completely
false",1))
question5.answers.append(RiskQuestionAnswer("Somewhat true",2))
question5.answers.append(RiskQuestionAnswer("Completely
true",3))
```

```
question6 = RiskQuestion("If you lose money investing today,
your current lifestyle would not be impacted.")
question6.answers.append(RiskQuestionAnswer("Completely
false",1))
question6.answers.append(RiskQuestionAnswer("Somewhat true",2))
question6.answers.append(RiskQuestionAnswer("Completely
true",3))


question7 = RiskQuestion("You do not need to draw down more
than 5% of your investment portfolio for any major financial
goal in the next five years.")
question7.answers.append(RiskQuestionAnswer("Completely
false",1))
question7.answers.append(RiskQuestionAnswer("Somewhat true",2))
question7.answers.append(RiskQuestionAnswer("Completely
true",3))


capacityQuestionnaire.questions.append(question4)
capacityQuestionnaire.questions.append(question5)
capacityQuestionnaire.questions.append(question6)
capacityQuestionnaire.questions.append(question7)
```

The idea here is very similar to what we did with our risk tolerance questionnaire, but the questions are now more focused on financial health.

While this method of manually creating the `Questionnaire` objects works, it seems more likely you would find it more productive to create a questionnaire in a database or a spreadsheet. So, let's use the same questions but place them in a spreadsheet that we can then read into our Python code. We will create two separate spreadsheets to organize and link the questions and answers. *Figure 7.1* shows the spreadsheet for questions:

QuestionID	QuestionType	QuestionText	QuestionWeight
1	Tolerance	In general, how would your best friend describe you as a risk taker?	2
2	Tolerance	You are on a TV game show and can choose one of the following. Which would you take?	1
3	Tolerance	When you think of the word risk which of the following words comes to mind first?	1
4	Capacity	You are able to save money regularly.	1
5	Capacity	You can pay all your monthly bills on time -- including any credit card or other debt.	1
6	Capacity	If you lose money investing today, your current lifestyle would not be impacted.	1
7	Capacity	You do not need to draw down more than 5% of your investment portfolio for any major financial goal in the next five years.	1

Figure 7.1 – Illustrative risk questions organized into a spreadsheet

Figure 7.2 shows the spreadsheet for answers:

AnswerID	AnswerText	AnswerValue	QuestionID
1	A real gambler	4	1
2	Willing to take risks after completing adequate research	3	1
3	Cautious	2	1
4	A real risk avoider	1	1
5	$1,000 in cash	1	2
6	A 50% chance at winning $5,000	2	2
7	A 25% chance at winning $10,000	3	2
8	A 5% chance at winning $100,000	4	2
9	Loss	1	3
10	Uncertainty	2	3
11	Opportunity	3	3
12	Thrill	4	3
13	Completely false	1	4
14	Somewhat true	2	4
15	Completely true	3	4
16	Completely false	1	5
17	Somewhat true	2	5
18	Completely true	3	5
19	Completely false	1	6
20	Somewhat true	2	6
21	Completely true	3	6
22	Completely false	1	7
23	Somewhat true	2	7
24	Completely true	3	7

Figure 7.2 – Corresponding answers to the questions in spreadsheet format

To read these two separate spreadsheets into our code, we will also need to join them using some additional code. The key here is QuestionID, which is present in both datasets and links them together. While we're at it, let's add this as a utility method within the RiskQuestionnaire class for easy access:

```
def loadQuestionnaire(self, riskQuestionsFileName,
    riskAnswersFileName, type):
  if not (type in ["Tolerance", "Capacity"]):
        raise ValueError('Type must be Tolerance or
            Capacity.')
  import pandas as pd
  riskQuestions = pd.read_csv(
      riskQuestionsFileName).reset_index()
  riskAnswers = pd.read_csv(
      riskAnswersFileName).reset_index()
  if (type == "Tolerance"):
    toleranceQuestions =
```

```
riskQuestions[(riskQuestions['QuestionType'] == 'Tolerance')].
reset_index()
    for index, row in toleranceQuestions.iterrows():
        self.questions.append(
            RiskQuestion(row['QuestionText'],
                         row['QuestionWeight']))
        answers = riskAnswers[(riskAnswers['QuestionID'] ==
            row['QuestionID'])]
        for indexA, rowA in answers.iterrows():
            self.questions[index].answers.append(
                RiskQuestionAnswer(rowA['AnswerText'],
                                   rowA['AnswerValue']))
    else:
        capacityQuestions = riskQuestions[(riskQuestions[
            'QuestionType'] == 'Capacity')].reset_index()
    for index, row in capacityQuestions.iterrows():
        self.questions.append(
            RiskQuestion(row['QuestionText'],
                         row['QuestionWeight']))
        answers = riskAnswers[(
            riskAnswers['QuestionID'] == row['QuestionID'])]
        for indexA, rowA in answers.iterrows():
            self.questions[index].answers.append(
                RiskQuestionAnswer(rowA['AnswerText'],
                                   rowA['AnswerValue']))
```

Okay, so we've used a few nifty pieces of Python magic to keep things simple. One is the reset_ index() method from pandas.DataFrame. This is useful to ensure that whichever DataFrame we're handling, the first-row index is zero and not something else that could be unpredictable. We're using another function called iterrows() that allows us to use a standard for loop to walk through our DataFrame row by row. Since we've made loadQuestionnaire a function of the class itself, we don't need to create a new object, but instead, use the self-reference to the class object that is already created.

To find the list of answers to each question, we're using something equivalent to the classic SQL WHERE operator, which works similarly to a standard If statement in DataFrames, where we reference a column in the DataFrame as the equivalence condition. If that seems confusing, try some toy examples, and you'll see what's happening. Finally, while we're still looping through our questions, we add a secondary loop through the answers adding them to our questionnaire in the right place.

To use our new fancy version of setting up a questionnaire, we just need to upload our files to Colab or Google Drive, and then we can do something like this:

```
questionsFileName = '/content/drive/MyDrive/Books/Robo-advisor
with Python /Data/Risk Questions.csv'
answersFileName = '/content/drive/MyDrive/Books/Robo-advisor
with Python /Data/Risk Answers.csv'

toleranceQuestionnaire = RiskQuestionnaire()
toleranceQuestionnaire.loadQuestionnaire(questionsFileName,
answersFileName, "Tolerance")

capacityQuestionnaire = RiskQuestionnaire()
capacityQuestionnaire.loadQuestionnaire(questionsFileName,
answersFileName, "Capacity")
```

Now that we have our two questionnaires created, we can print them out to see whether the correct format is maintained:

```
print("Risk Tolerance: \n")
for question in toleranceQuestionnaire.questions:
  print(question.questionText)
  for answer in question.answers:
    print(" -" + answer.answerText)
  print("\n")
```

You should see a printout like this:

```
Risk Tolerance:


In general, how would your best friend describe you as a risk
taker?
-A real gambler
-Willing to take risks after completing adequate research
-Cautious
-A real risk avoider


You are on a TV game show and can choose one of the following.
Which would you take?
-$1,000 in cash
```

```
-A 50% chance at winning $5,000
-A 25% chance at winning $10,000
-A 5% chance at winning $100,000


When you think of the word risk which of the following words
comes to mind first?
-Loss
-Uncertainty
-Opportunity
-Thrill
```

Now let's do the other one:

```
print("Risk Capacity: \n")
for question in capacityQuestionnaire.questions:
  print(question.questionText)
  for answer in question.answers:
    print(" -" + answer.answerText)
  print("\n")
```

You should see a printout like this:

```
Risk Capacity:


You are able to save money regularly.
-Completely false
-Somewhat true
-Completely true


You can pay all your monthly bills on time -- including any
credit card or other debt.
-Completely false
-Somewhat true
-Completely true


If you lose money investing today, your current lifestyle would
not be impacted.
-Completely false
-Somewhat true
```

```
-Completely true
```

```
You do not need to draw down more than 5% of your investment
portfolio for any major financial goal in the next five years.
-Completely false
-Somewhat true
-Completely true
```

Now, to provide our answers, we could just set them manually for each question, as follows:

```
toleranceQuestionnaire.questions[0].answers[1].selected = True
toleranceQuestionnaire.questions[1].answers[0].selected = True
toleranceQuestionnaire.questions[2].answers[2].selected = True

capacityQuestionnaire.questions[0].answers[1].selected = True
capacityQuestionnaire.questions[1].answers[1].selected = True
capacityQuestionnaire.questions[2].answers[2].selected = True
capacityQuestionnaire.questions[3].answers[1].selected = True
```

Technically, this gives us everything we need for now. While we aren't building a UI for our Robo-advisor in this book, we could also look at a more interactive way to fill in the questionnaire. We can do this by bundling the code thus far into a method that uses the Python console inside Google Colab to present questions and gather answers one by one, as follows:

```
def answerQuestionnaire(self):
    for i in range(len(self.questions)):
        question = self.questions[i]
        print(question.questionText)
        for n in range(len(question.answers)):
            answer = question.answers[n]
            print(str(n) + ": " + answer.answerText)
        nChosen = int(input("Choose your answer between 0 and " +
            str(len(question.answers)-1) + ": "))
        self.questions[i].answers[nChosen].selected = True
        print("\n")
```

Note that I've added this again as a class method under `RiskQuestionnaire`, but for the sake of space, I've omitted the full definition. Go ahead and just add this to the previous code block. Remember that in order to use this new code, you have to execute the whole class definition again and re-run the code to load the questionnaire from the file. Otherwise, you'll see an error that the `answerQuestionnaire` method isn't found.

The cool thing is that this method actually becomes super short and sweet due to the groundwork we've created and the structure of the classes we've used. Python has a useful `input()` method, which will pause the execution to show the user one field to fill in at a time, which we then convert into an integer and store in our `self` object. So, let's run this again and now add the answer method on top:

```
questionsFileName = '/content/drive/MyDrive/Books/Robo-advisor
with Python /Data/Risk Questions.csv'
answersFileName = '/content/drive/MyDrive/Books/Robo-advisor
with Python /Data/Risk Answers.csv'

toleranceQuestionnaire = RiskQuestionnaire()
toleranceQuestionnaire.loadQuestionnaire(questionsFileName,
answersFileName, "Tolerance")

capacityQuestionnaire = RiskQuestionnaire()
capacityQuestionnaire.loadQuestionnaire(questionsFileName,
answersFileName, "Capacity")

toleranceQuestionnaire.answerQuestionnaire()
capacityQuestionnaire.answerQuestionnaire()
```

You should see something like this:

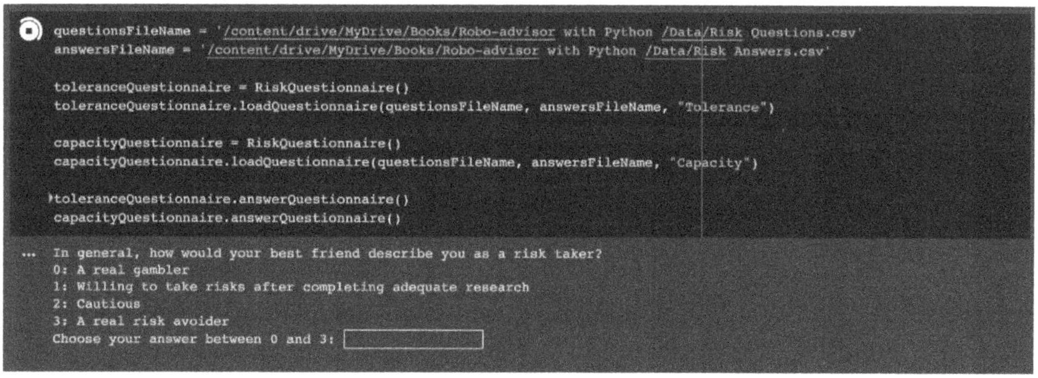

Figure 7.3 – Example of running our interactive questionnaire in Google Colab

That wraps up our exploration of creating risk questionnaires. Certainly, this is not exhaustive. There is a wide range of methodologies and theories about risk profiling, and entire companies are dedicated to creating risk questions. Our example of risk capacity covered only financial health, but you may find other examples online that cover other relevant factors such as time horizon, what type of Goal we're investing in, and what the investor's experience is with the relevant investment products on offer.

At the end of the day, it is your responsibility to choose a methodology and build your own questionnaires. The local regulations will dictate what is allowed and what is recommended based on regulatory guidelines issued by the relevant government authority.

For us, the only thing missing now is a risk score, which we will calculate next.

Calculating a risk score

To round out this chapter, we will add one final method to our growing `RiskQuestionnaire` class:

```
def calculateScore(self):
  print("Risk Score:")
  myTotalScore = 0
  for question in self.questions:
    for answer in question.answers:
      if (answer.selected == True):
        myTotalScore = myTotalScore + (
            answer.score * question.weight)
        print(answer.answerText + ": " + str(
            answer.score * question.weight))
  print("Total Risk Score: " + str(myTotalScore) + "\n")
```

In our case, this is very straightforward. We simply add up the weighted sum of each answer to create a score. Certainly, far more advanced and complex solutions are possible for determining risk scores, but I will leave this with you to determine the appropriate solution for your investors.

As before, you'll now need to re-run the code that creates and answers our risk questionnaires to use this new class method:

```
toleranceQuestionnaire.calculateScore()
capacityQuestionnaire.calculateScore()
```

You should see the following output, obviously depending on how you answered the questions:

```
Risk Score:
Willing to take risks after completing adequate research: 6
$1,000 in cash: 1
Opportunity: 3
Total Risk Score: 10
```

```
Risk Score:
Somewhat true: 2
Somewhat true: 2
Completely true: 3
Somewhat true: 2
Total Risk Score: 9
```

In this instance, we have a risk tolerance of 10 out of 16 and a risk capacity of 9 out of 12. Typically, this would imply that we are a moderate growth investor, coming somewhere in the upper middle of the range. Of course, this isn't conclusive until we have portfolios to map our risk scores. That will allow us to ultimately end up with an investment allocation appropriate to our perceived level of risk. This will have to wait until the next chapter, as we must first build some portfolios.

Summary

This chapter added another core capability to our Robo-advisor toolkit. We started by revising some key terminology for risk profiling in risk tolerance, risk capacity, and risk scores. We then proceeded to create our first risk questionnaire by creating the necessary objects to store this information.

First, we took some illustrative example questions from online sources for risk tolerance and risk capacity. From there, we added a key ability to read questions and answers from a spreadsheet to load into our Python code, giving us greater flexibility in modifying our questionnaire when needed.

To complete our required capabilities, we also added an interactive program to answer those questions in Google Colab, making the experience more dynamic. Finally, we added one last helper method to our main `RiskQuestionnaire` class to calculate a risk score based on our answers. This we will keep for later.

Now, let's proceed to the beating heart of a Robo-advisor: the portfolio. In the next chapter, we will finally look at what type of investments our Robo-advisor could make on behalf of the investors.

Further reading

You might be interested in reading some extra information related to the topics discussed in this chapter. Here are a few links to some of the external resources:

- Grable, John & Lytton, Ruth. *Financial risk tolerance revisited: The development of a risk assessment instrument*. Financial Services Review, vol. 8, 1999, pp. 163-181

- *RBC Global Asset Management. Quiz: What is your risk capacity?* Accessed online 15.10.2022: `https://www.rbcgam.com/en/ca/learn-plan/investment-basics/whats-your-risk-capacity/detail`

8

Model Portfolio Construction

In this chapter, we will finally choose what kind of investments our Robo-advisor will be making on behalf of investors. We will make good use of several handy Python modules to speed up our work rather than building everything up from scratch. We will add capabilities to a core `Portfolio` class as we go along, starting from some basic properties but then adding market data, portfolio construction, and finally, mapping to our risk scores from the previous chapter.

By the end of this chapter, you should have a clear understanding of how portfolios are constructed within the context of a typical Robo-advisor. You should have all the skills required to implement portfolio capabilities for your own Robo-advisor project using Python.

In this chapter, we're going to cover the following topics:

- Learning about the key concepts of modern portfolio theory
- Creating your first portfolio
- Analyzing the makeup of your portfolio
- Creating multiple portfolios using risk bands
- Mapping model portfolios to risk scores
- Learning about the differences between self-directed and managed portfolios

Learning about the key concepts of modern portfolio theory (MPT)

What did Harry Markowitz tell us about managing our portfolios? While it may seem somewhat obvious that for any investment, you would want to maximize your investment returns while taking minimal risks, the challenge is implementing that in practice. This is what MPT provides us—a practical framework for calculating risk and using it to determine an optimal makeup for our portfolio. Markowitz makes a number of famous assumptions in his paper, the first of which is called **diversification**. It simply means that to find a balance between risk and reward, your portfolio should contain different types of investments: some high-risk, high-reward; some low–risk low-reward. To make this actionable, he chooses the metric of correlation to determine whether investments are different or not.

According to MPT, if we assume a portfolio of multiple potential investments, to find our optimal portfolio, we need three inputs:

- **Expected returns**: This is a simple weighted sum of the average annualized returns for each investment in the portfolio. It is a proxy for how much return we should expect in the future from these investments.

- **Variance**: Markowitz's choice of proxy for calculating risk is how much variance the returns of the investment have shown, which means are they stable or wildly fluctuating. In finance, when measured over a period of time, this is typically called **volatility** instead. The square root of variance is the **standard deviation**.

- **Correlation**: Using the previous metrics of return and variance, we can calculate the covariance between investments in the portfolio, which indicates whether the investments are moving up or down in unison, in opposite directions, or randomly.

Using these inputs, we can then calculate the following:

- **Efficient Frontier**: This is an optimization method that allows us to minimize the amount of risk we take in our portfolio in relation to returns.

- **Sharpe Ratio**: While Markowitz wanted to optimize for minimal volatility, it is common to instead optimize for the Sharpe ratio, which is a measure of how much returns improve for a given increase in risk. The formula for the Sharpe ratio is as follows:

$$S = \frac{R_p - R_f}{\sigma}$$

Where:

- R_p is our target portfolio's return
- R_f the risk-free rate
- σ is the standard deviation of the portfolio's return above the risk-free rate

- **Risk Band**: This is a number to indicate the relative risk within a selection of model portfolios. If your Robo-advisor has five portfolios, then you would have five corresponding risk bands from 1-5, with 1 indicating the lowest risk portfolio, and 5 indicating the highest risk portfolio.

Now that we've got our basic terminology straight, we can start piecing things together for capabilities needed for our portfolios.

Creating your first portfolio

Now let's start by setting up some basic classes to capture and store information about portfolios:

```python
class Portfolio:
    def __init__(self, name, riskBucket, expectedReturn=0,
    expectedRisk=0):
        self.name = name
        self.riskBucket = riskBucket
        self.allocations = []
        self.expectedReturn = expectedReturn
        self.expectedRisk = expectedRisk


class Allocation:
    def __init__(self, ticker, percentage):
        self.ticker = ticker
        self.percentage = percentage
```

In this example implementation, we've stored key MPT properties in `expectedReturn` and `expectedRisk`. Additionally, we've added the `riskBucket` property to capture some information about the relative level of risk between our different portfolios. Finally, we added a list of objects belonging to the `Allocation` class that will store the constituent investment products that make up our portfolio. Let's create our first portfolio:

```python
stocks = Allocation("SPY", 0.6)
bonds = Allocation("TLT", 0.4)
myPortfolio = Portfolio("Growth", 4)
myPortfolio.allocations.append(stocks)
myPortfolio.allocations.append(bonds)
```

In this example, we've chosen two of the most popular US ETFs: SPDR S&P 500 Trust ETF (`SPY`) and iShares 20+ Year Treasury Bond ETF (`TLT`). The first represents the equity component, and the latter fixed income. This type of *60/40* portfolio is one of the more popular portfolios due to its simplicity and diversification as an all-round portfolio applicable in most situations.

Now that we have our first portfolio, it's time to examine its contents. This is typically necessary information to share with investors that are considering investment in the portfolio you have created.

Analyzing the makeup of your portfolio

As we learned from Markowitz, the basis of constructing any portfolio should be proper diversification. In practice, this typically means diversification along multiple dimensions of potential investment products, such as the following:

- **Asset class**: This is just a way to separate different types of investible assets, the classics being stocks, bonds, and commodities. One can get as granular as one likes, of course. While regulations currently limit the inclusion of cryptocurrencies, which seem a likely addition to future portfolios sooner rather than later.

- **Asset region**: Another popular method of diversification is to choose investments from different countries. Typically, one would have varying degrees of exposure to the main market groups such as America, Europe, Asia, and an evolving group named emerging markets.

- **Asset industry**: Given the humongous impact of tech stocks in recent decades, it makes sense to diversify into other more traditional industries when tech dominates many indexes such as S&P 500 and NASDAQ 100. There is a plethora of funds dedicated to obvious and niche industries, from energy and consumer goods to biotech and robotics.

- **Currency**: While this would not have much impact on an American Robo-advisor operating in America, it is a more complex issue for markets with less stable currencies and low availability of local currency investment products. In certain cases, it may be necessary to combine US dollar products with locally denominated products to hedge against bias and volatility against the US dollar, especially if your income and spending is in local currency. Differences in taxation may also need to be addressed when choosing products.

- **Fees**: While not necessary for the purposes of diversification directly, commonly used criteria for product selection are fees. Some popular products such as ETFs range from a small fraction of one percent in annual fees, but certain mutual funds can have complicated fee schedules that also place limitations on how and when you can sell them for profit. Generally speaking, the tendency is to prefer high-volume low-cost ETF providers.

To build our portfolios, we would feed in a selection of products using the factors listed here. To construct a typical set of 4-5 Robo-advisor model portfolios, you would start from a product universe of 10-20 products. The more products you add, the more transactions you will generate down the line, potentially generating more fees and overhead.

Now let's analyze our portfolio. We will be analyzing our portfolio along three dimensions: asset class, asset region, and asset industry. Let's start with asset class:

```
import matplotlib.pyplot as plt
import numpy as np

assetClassWeights = [myPortfolio.allocations[0].percentage,
```

```
myPortfolio.allocations[1].percentage]
assetClassLabels = ["Stocks", "Bonds"]

plt.pie(assetClassWeights, labels = assetClassLabels)
plt.show()
```

Here, we make use of `pyplot` to generate a nice pie chart. You will see something like this:

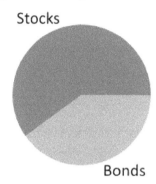

Figure 8.1 – Illustrative portfolio breakdown by asset class

Now let's move on to asset region, to create something similar. To do that, we'll first install the `yfinance` module, which we tried out in *Chapter 5*:

```
!pip install yfinance
import yfinance as yf
```

Assuming that code runs without any issues, let's re-create our portfolio using `yfinance` to get some data on these products:

```
spy = yf.Ticker("SPY")
tlt = yf.Ticker("TLT")
spy.info
```

This will print out a long output of information about the SPY ETF – a lot more than we will need, in fact. You should see something like this:

```
{'exchange': 'PCX', 'shortName': 'SPDR S&P 500', 'longName':
'SPDR S&P 500 ETF Trust', 'exchangeTimezoneName': 'America/New_
York', 'exchangeTimezoneShortName': 'EST', 'isEsgPopulated':
False, 'gmtOffSetMilliseconds': '-18000000', 'quoteType':
'ETF', 'symbol': 'SPY', 'messageBoardId': 'finmb_6160262',
```

```
'market': 'us_market', 'annualHoldingsTurnover': None,
'enterpriseToRevenue': None, 'beta3Year': 1, 'profitMargins':
None, 'enterpriseToEbitda': None, '52WeekChange': None,
'morningStarRiskRating': None, 'forwardEps': None,
'revenueQuarterlyGrowth': None, 'fundInceptionDate': 727660800,
'annualReportExpenseRatio': None, 'totalAssets': 386065727488,
'bookValue': None, 'fundFamily': 'SPDR State Street Global
Advisors', ...
```

Now we can use some of that information for generating a region breakdown:

```
import pandas as pd
stockMarket = spy.info["market"]
bondMarket = tlt.info["market"]


df = pd.DataFrame([[stockMarket, myPortfolio.allocations[0].
percentage], [bondMarket, myPortfolio.allocations[1].
percentage]])
df = df.groupby(0).sum().reset_index()


assetClassWeights = [df.loc[0][1]]
assetClassLabels = [df.loc[0][0]]


plt.pie(assetClassWeights, labels = assetClassLabels)
plt.show()
```

Here, we reference a single attribute of the info object from yfinance, which gives us only the market information we're after. To ensure we see only one line or slice per region, we need to use the groupby function from DataFrame, with the addition of a sum function to ensure that we add together percentages for the same regions. The output is displayed in the following figure:

us_market

Figure 8.2 – Illustrative portfolio breakdown by asset region

Depending on where we intend to present this information, we might choose to clean up the formatting, to show something like **US** instead of **us_market**. These kinds of formatting questions will obviously depend on the source of your data.

Now let's move on to the asset industry following the same method:

```
sectors1 = spy.info["sectorWeightings"]
sectors2 = tlt.info["sectorWeightings"]

df = pd.DataFrame(sectors1)
df2 = pd.DataFrame(sectors2)
df = df.append(df2)
df.index.name = "index"

df = df.groupby("index", dropna=True).sum().sum().reset_index()

sectorWeights = df[df.columns[1]]
sectorLabels = df[df.columns[0]]

plt.pie(sectorWeights, labels = sectorLabels)
plt.show()
```

Now, this might seem a little magical, but oftentimes, when dealing with tabular data, you will need to play around and experiment with various ways to extract the data that you need in the format that you need. First, we combine two tables from the two products in our portfolio using the `append` function. Here, we again use the `groupby` function but now we use two `sum` functions to end up with a table that we can present in a pie chart. This is what we get:

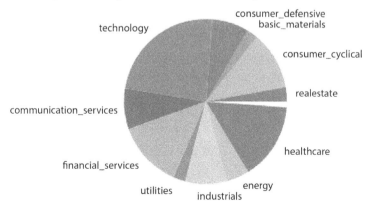

Figure 8.3 – Illustrative portfolio breakdown by asset industry

If we wanted, we could easily clean this up a little by replacing the underscore characters with spaces and capitalizing each word:

```
for index, value in sectorLabels.iteritems():
  sectorLabels[index] = (value.capitalize().replace("_", " "))


plt.pie(sectorWeights, labels = sectorLabels)
plt.show()
```

If we go through each of the industry sector labels, we can then use the `capitalize` and `replace` functions on each string to get the result we wanted, as shown in the following screenshot:

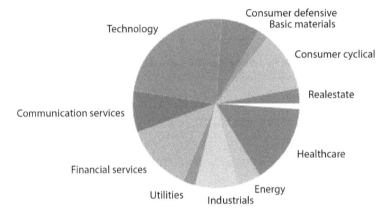

Figure 8.4 – Illustrative portfolio breakdown by asset industry, with cleaned up formatting

Now that we've covered the basics of creating a single portfolio, we will move on to the more advanced aspects of MPT and create multiple portfolios using the efficient frontier model.

Creating multiple portfolios using risk bands

Before we can get to the MPT-specific concerns, we need to get some market data and format it specifically for the modules we will be using. If you end up using different modules or writing your own efficient frontier code, you may need different data formatting. Now, let's download some market data:

```
df = yf.download("SPY TLT",group_by="Ticker",period="20y")
df
```

We just need one simple command to download a lot of data, in fact, daily prices for 20 years for the two ETFs in our portfolios. To see what we got, you can simply run the DataFrame object by calling `df`. We should see something like this:

Date	SPY						TLT					
	Open	High	Low	Close	Adj Close	Volume	Open	High	Low	Close	Adj Close	Volume
2002-09-23	83.650002	84.059998	82.690002	83.660004	56.980827	46893800	90.000000	90.239998	89.769997	90.099998	46.215858	163200
2002-09-24	82.440002	83.650002	81.849998	82.309998	56.061359	69507000	90.300003	90.940002	90.209999	90.680000	46.513332	251900
2002-09-25	83.370003	84.769997	82.040001	84.349998	57.450809	59294400	90.099998	90.360001	89.260002	89.580002	45.949120	127200
2002-09-26	85.019997	85.970001	84.449997	85.730003	58.390717	53638000	89.050003	89.529999	88.610001	89.370003	45.841362	429000
2002-09-27	85.000000	85.629997	82.750000	82.750000	56.361046	64648300	89.529999	90.040001	89.480003	90.040001	46.185051	298200
...	...	...	...	...	...	...	...	...	...	...	...	...
2022-09-19	382.260010	388.549988	382.179993	388.549988	388.549988	73278500	106.959999	107.820000	106.800003	107.320000	107.320000	11084400
2022-09-20	385.059998	386.119995	381.200012	384.089996	384.089996	77274900	105.690002	106.839996	105.400002	106.250000	106.250000	20133800
2022-09-21	386.109985	389.309998	377.380005	377.390015	377.390015	106746600	106.699997	108.040001	105.970001	108.029999	108.029999	23132900
2022-09-22	376.579987	378.299988	373.440002	374.220001	374.220001	89343100	105.790001	105.959999	104.730003	105.269997	105.269997	29017700
2022-09-23	370.579987	370.589996	367.429993	367.869202	367.869202	23232717	105.339996	105.539902	104.934998	105.309998	105.309998	4188163

5037 rows × 12 columns

Figure 8.5 – A sample of our first market data

We can see that the resulting DataFrame has an interesting structure with two layers of columns. We have various numeric values for both `SPY` and `TLT` one after another, organized by the date as the index. What we need is simpler, since we're only interested in closing prices for each day. So, let's clean this up a bit:

```
df = df.iloc[:, df.columns.get_level_values(1)=="Close"]
df = df.dropna()
df.columns = df.columns.droplevel(1)
df
```

These few lines of code, in order, will first get rid of all the other columns besides `Close`, delete any rows for which we have no price data, and finally, leave us with the product name in place of the closing price to keep it neat. The reason we want to delete any rows with empty data is that you may have investment products in your portfolio that were published in different years. For example, if you want 20 years of data, you should be sure that those products were actually created more than 20 years ago. If you have one ETF that was created last year, you won't have enough data. You will get an output similar to the following:

	SPY	TLT
Date		
2002-09-23	83.660004	90.099998
2002-09-24	82.309998	90.680000
2002-09-25	84.349998	89.580002
2002-09-26	85.730003	89.370003
2002-09-27	82.750000	90.040001
...	...	...
2022-09-19	388.549988	107.320000
2022-09-20	384.089996	106.250000
2022-09-21	377.390015	108.029999
2022-09-22	374.220001	105.269997
2022-09-23	367.869202	105.309998

5037 rows × 2 columns

Figure 8.6 – Our cleaned up market data

Let's go ahead and add all this useful code as a class method as we've done in previous chapters. This will all go under Portfolio:

```
class Portfolio:
  def __init__(self, name, riskBucket, expectedReturn=0,
    expectedRisk=0):
    self.name = name
    self.riskBucket = riskBucket
    self.allocations = []
    self.expectedReturn = expectedReturn
    self.expectedRisk = expectedRisk

  def getDailyPrices(self, period):
    tickerStringList = ""
    for allocation in self.allocations:
      tickerStringList = tickerStringList + str(
          allocation.ticker) + " "
    data = yf.download(tickerStringList, group_by="Ticker",
        period=period)
    data = data.iloc[:,
```

```
        data.columns.get_level_values(1)=="Close"]
    data = data.dropna()
    data.columns = data.columns.droplevel(1)
    return data
```

Now we can access the allocations that we've already defined and format them as required by the download function within `yfinance`. Let's try this out:

```
stocks = Allocation("SPY", 0.6)
bonds = Allocation("TLT", 0.4)
myPortfolio = Portfolio("Growth", 4)
myPortfolio.allocations.append(stocks)
myPortfolio.allocations.append(bonds)
df = myPortfolio.getDailyPrices("20y")
```

The contents of `df` should be similar to what we got before in *Figure 8.5*. This gives us all we need to move on to building an efficient frontier. To do that, we'll be using another module called `PyPortfolioOpt`. This lets us get what we need without needing to implement all the math ourselves. However, if you do wish to do exactly that, one good source might be *Python For Finance* (Yan). We'll use the following command to install `PyPortfolioOpt`:

```
!pip install PyPortfolioOpt
```

This gives us all the tools needed to calculate an efficient frontier for any given portfolio. Let's give it a whirl:

```
from pypfopt.efficient_frontier import EfficientFrontier
from pypfopt import risk_models
from pypfopt import expected_returns

mu = expected_returns.mean_historical_return(df)
S = risk_models.sample_cov(df)

ef = EfficientFrontier(mu, S)
weights = ef.max_sharpe()
ef.portfolio_performance(verbose=True)
```

In just a few lines of code, we can use our price history data stored in the DataFrame variable `df`, and find the portfolio weights to maximize the Sharpe ratio. The resulting output would be similar to this:

```
Expected annual return: 7.2%
Annual volatility: 18.9%
```

```
Sharpe Ratio: 0.27
(0.07185955933782329, 0.18883916007480855, 0.2746229082849084)
```

One indication that our portfolio might not be that well diversified is that the resulting Sharpe ratio is quite low and volatility is quite high. We can check the optimized weights of our two constituent ETFs with this command:

```
ef.clean_weights()
```

You should see something like this:

```
OrderedDict([('SPY', 0.87679), ('TLT', 0.12321)])
```

We can visualize the result using the same Python module that we used earlier:

```
import matplotlib.pyplot as plt
from pypfopt import plotting
fig, ax = plt.subplots()
ef = EfficientFrontier(mu, S)
plotting.plot_efficient_frontier(ef, ax=ax, show_assets=True)
plt.show()
```

You will get an output that looks something like this:

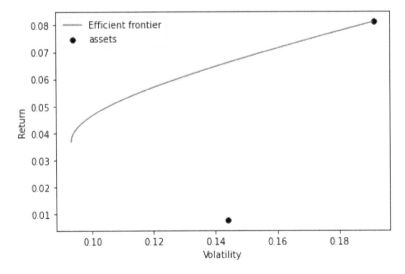

Figure 8.7 – Example efficient frontier for our portfolio

Obviously, it's not a very interesting graph to look at with just two assets, but you get the idea. So, that yields just one portfolio, but we need more than that for our Robo-advisor. Typically, you would choose a number of risk bands, say between 5 and 10, and build portfolios to correspond to certain target returns. Let's see that in practice. Instead of simply one portfolio that maximizes the Sharpe ratio, we can extract a portfolio targeting a return. For the sake of this exercise, let's pick nice even numbers and set constraints for 2%, 4%, 6%, 8%, and 10% returns using the efficient_return method within PyPortfolioOpt:

```
ef = EfficientFrontier(mu, S)
ef.efficient_return(0.02)
portfolio1 = ef.clean_weights()
print(portfolio1)
ef.efficient_return(0.04)
portfolio2 = ef.clean_weights()
print(portfolio2)
ef.efficient_return(0.06)
portfolio3 = ef.clean_weights()
print(portfolio3)
ef.efficient_return(0.08)
portfolio4 = ef.clean_weights()
print(portfolio4)
ef.efficient_return(0.10)
portfolio5 = ef.clean_weights()
print(portfolio5)
```

Now, in most cases, this should actually fail because the portfolio will struggle to produce a 10% return. You should see something like this:

```
OrderedDict([('SPY', 0.39178), ('TLT', 0.60822)])
OrderedDict([('SPY', 0.46059), ('TLT', 0.53941)])
OrderedDict([('SPY', 0.74579), ('TLT', 0.25421)])
---------------------------------------------------------------
ValueError                          Traceback (most recent call last)
<ipython-input-7-20d666e38688> in <module>
     11 portfolio1 = ef.clean_weights()
     12 print(portfolio1)
---> 13 ef.efficient_return(0.08)
     14 portfolio1 = ef.clean_weights()
```

```
15 print(portfolio1)
```

```
/usr/local/lib/python3.7/dist-packages/pypfopt/efficient_
frontier/efficient_frontier.py in efficient_return(self,
target_return, market_neutral)
    396             if target_return > self._max_return_value:
    397                 raise ValueError(
--> 398                     "target_return must be lower than the
maximum possible return"
    399                 )
    400
```

**ValueError: target_return must be lower than the maximum
possible return**

In this instance, it already fails at 8% returns. So, we would either need to lower our return expectations or find another portfolio. We can try the latter as an example, by imagining a portfolio with further bias toward high-growth tech stocks. This is probably not a good idea for a real-life portfolio due to concentration risk and huge volatility, but it will demonstrate that it is possible. To clarify, in most regulations, you will be forbidden from using any other products besides listed ETF funds for your Robo-advisor. First, let's make further improvements to our Portfolio class to add all this as part of our class methods:

```
class Portfolio:

  def __init__(self, tickerString: str, expectedReturn: float,
    portfolioName: str, riskBucket: int):
    self.name = portfolioName
    self.riskBucket = riskBucket
    self.expectedReturn = expectedReturn
    self.allocations = []

    from pypfopt.efficient_frontier import EfficientFrontier
    from pypfopt import risk_models
    from pypfopt import expected_returns

    df = self.__getDailyPrices(tickerString, "20y")

    mu = expected_returns.mean_historical_return(df)
```

```
S = risk_models.sample_cov(df)

ef = EfficientFrontier(mu, S)

ef.efficient_return(expectedReturn)
self.expectedRisk = ef.portfolio_performance()[1]
portfolioWeights = ef.clean_weights()

for key, value in portfolioWeights.items():
    newAllocation = Allocation(key, value)
    self.allocations.append(newAllocation)
```

The beauty of this approach is that now the constructor method itself does most of the work, including assigning our risk property and filling in our portfolio allocations. Now we should also update the class methods:

```
def __getDailyPrices(self, tickerStringList, period):
    data = yf.download(tickerStringList, group_by="Ticker",
        period=period)
    data = data.iloc[:,
        data.columns.get_level_values(1)=="Close"]
    data = data.dropna()
    data.columns = data.columns.droplevel(1)
    return data


def printPortfolio(self):
    print("Portfolio Name: " + self.name)
    print("Risk Bucket: " + str(self.riskBucket))
    print("Expected Return: " + str(self.expectedReturn))
    print("Expected Risk: " + str(self.expectedRisk))
    print("Allocations: ")
    for allocation in self.allocations:
        print("Ticker: " + allocation.ticker + ",
            Percentage: " + str(allocation.percentage))
```

Notice how we have set the __getDailyPrices method as a private class method by using the double underscore prefix. This comes in handy when you need helper methods that only make sense in the context of some internal class operation, and not as a standalone method worth exposing outside the class. We also add a handy printPortfolio method to show us the portfolio we've built. Let's see this in action:

```
myPortfolio = Portfolio("SPY TLT AAPL AMZN NFLX GOOGL MSFT",
expectedReturn = 0.10, portfolioName = "Aggressive Growth",
riskBucket = 5)
myPortfolio.printPortfolio()
```

This will yield the following output:

```
[*********************100%**********************]   7 of 7
completed
Portfolio Name: Aggressive Growth
Risk Bucket: 5
Expected Return: 0.1
Expected Risk: 0.11036746588621268
Allocations:
Ticker: GOOGL, Percentage: 0.0625
Ticker: NFLX, Percentage: 0.03181
Ticker: SPY, Percentage: 0.15241
Ticker: TLT, Percentage: 0.56974
Ticker: MSFT, Percentage: 0.0
Ticker: AAPL, Percentage: 0.17176
Ticker: AMZN, Percentage: 0.01179
```

In this illustrative example, we see the main drivers of the portfolio end up being the fixed-income ETF TLT, our trusty S&P500 ETF SPY, and the Apple stock. We can now visualize this portfolio once again but using a bit more flair. If we add two additional properties, self.mu and self.S, to our Portfolio class constructor, we can add the following helper method to show our efficient frontier:

```
def showEfficientFrontier(self):
    import numpy as np
    ef = EfficientFrontier(self.mu, self.S)
    fig, ax = plt.subplots()
    ef_max_sharpe = EfficientFrontier(self.mu, self.S)
```

```
ef_return = EfficientFrontier(self.mu, self.S)
plotting.plot_efficient_frontier(ef, ax=ax,
    show_assets=False)
n_samples = 10000
w = np.random.dirichlet(np.ones(ef.n_assets), n_samples)
rets = w.dot(ef.expected_returns)
stds = np.sqrt(np.diag(w @ ef.cov_matrix @ w.T))
sharpes = rets / stds
ax.scatter(stds, rets, marker=".", c=sharpes,
    cmap="viridis_r")
ef_max_sharpe.max_sharpe()
ret_tangent, std_tangent, _ =
    ef_max_sharpe.portfolio_performance()
ax.scatter(std_tangent, ret_tangent, marker="*", s=100,
    c="r", label="Max Sharpe")
ef_return.efficient_return(self.expectedReturn)
ret_tangent2, std_tangent2, _ =
    ef_return.portfolio_performance()
returnP = str(int(self.expectedReturn*100))+"%"
ax.scatter(std_tangent2, ret_tangent2, marker="*", s=100,
    c="y", label=returnP)
ax.set_title("Efficient Frontier for " + returnP +
    " returns")
ax.legend()
plt.tight_layout()
plt.show()
```

Here, we add three interesting elements to our chart: the best portfolio for the highest Sharpe ratio, the portfolio for our target returns, and then 10,000 random portfolios to show the range of possibilities available in between. The output of myPortfolio.showEfficientFrontier() will look like this:

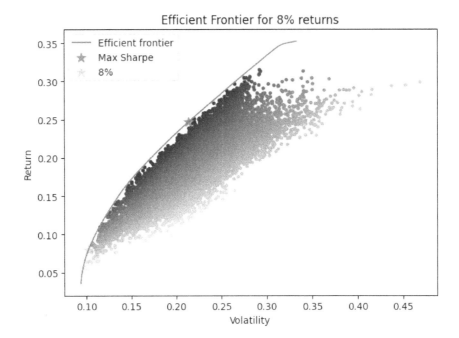

Figure 8.8 – Our fancy efficient frontier example

For the sake of completeness, you would, of course, need to generate portfolios for each risk bucket. I will leave that as an exercise for you once you have chosen your products and target characteristics for your portfolios.

Now that we have the ability to generate portfolios using the efficient frontier, we can start putting it all together to map our risk scores from *Chapter 7*, *Risk Profiling and Scoring*, to our portfolios.

Mapping model portfolios to risk scores

Now we will stitch together two major capabilities that we have built for our Robo-advisor: risk profiling and model portfolios. The link between the two is the risk score(s) that we get from the risk questionnaire as an output and the risk buckets that define our portfolios. Here is a visual example from Charles Schwab I found online (Schwab).

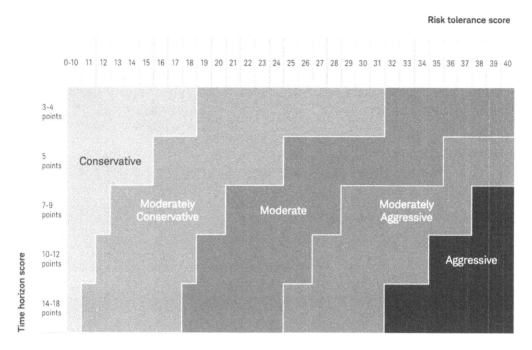

Figure 8.9 – Illustrative risk mapping table from Charles Schwab

The basic idea is that we set up a table that includes potential ranges for our risk tolerance and risk capacity scores, and decide the boundaries between our risk buckets as a function of those two values. Here, in place of risk capacity, we have a simple time horizon test, and in place of risk buckets, we simply see the implied portfolio names. We can construct something similar on the basis of our illustrative risk questionnaire from *Chapter 7*.

Risk Tolerance	Risk Capacity								
	4	5	6	7	8	9	10	11	12
4-6	1	2	2	2	2	2	3	3	3
7-9	1	2	2	2	2	2	3	3	4
10-12	1	2	2	2	2	3	3	4	4
13-15	1	2	2	2	3	3	4	4	5
16	1	2	2	3	3	3	4	5	5

Figure 8.10 – Illustrative risk mapping table

The illustrative risk questionnaires we came up with for risk tolerance and risk capacity had different potential minimum and maximum ranges for scores based on the answers chosen. Therefore, following the example from Schwab, we would need to decide how many portfolios we wish to create. In our preceding code, we imagined that number to be five, so let's use that here. That gives us one risk bucket for each portfolio: one to five.

Now, we must simply decide which combination of risk tolerance and risk capacity scores is suitable for each one of those five portfolios. As in the Schwab example, the general direction is going to be starting at portfolio one in the top-left corner, representing low risk, and proceeding diagonally toward the bottom right, representing high risk. The specific decisions on those boundaries are left as an exercise to you, depending on your specific decisions about risk questionnaires, portfolios, and local regulations. This risk mapping table is likely subject to regulatory approvals.

In order to use this table for our code, it's better to organize it as a lookup table, as shown in the following example. It is fundamentally the same data, but more easily digestible in code.

Portfolio	Capacity_min	Capacity_max	Tolerance_min	Tolerance_max
1	0	10	4	6
1	0	10	7	9
1	0	10	10	12
1	0	10	13	15
1	0	10	16	16
2	11	20	4	6
2	11	20	7	9
2	11	20	10	12
2	11	20	13	15
2	11	20	16	16
2	21	30	4	6
2	21	30	7	9
2	21	30	10	12
2	21	30	13	15
2	21	30	16	16
2	31	40	4	6
2	31	40	7	9
2	31	40	10	12
2	31	40	13	15
3	31	40	16	16
2	41	50	4	6
2	41	50	7	9
2	41	50	10	12
3	41	50	13	15
3	41	50	16	16
2	51	60	4	6
2	51	60	7	9
3	51	60	10	12
3	51	60	13	15
3	51	60	16	16
3	61	70	4	6
3	61	70	7	9
3	61	70	10	12
4	61	70	13	15
4	61	70	16	16
3	71	80	4	6
3	71	80	7	9
4	71	80	10	12
4	71	80	13	15
4	71	80	16	16
3	81	90	4	6
4	81	90	7	9
4	81	90	10	12
5	81	90	13	15
5	81	90	16	16
3	91	100	4	6
4	91	100	7	9
4	91	100	10	12
5	91	100	13	15
5	91	100	16	16

Figure 8.11 – Illustrative risk mapping lookup table

Let's look at a way to read this table into our code. Again, we will reuse our existing `Portfolio` class, and add another class method:

```
@staticmethod
  def getPortfolioMapping(riskToleranceScore,
riskCapacityScore):
      import pandas as pd
      allocationLookupTable=pd.read_csv('/content/drive/MyDrive/
Books/Robo-advisor with Python /Data/Allocation Lookup.csv')
      matchTol = (allocationLookupTable['Tolerance_min']
<=  riskToleranceScore) & (allocationLookupTable['Tolerance_
max'] >=  riskToleranceScore)
      matchCap = (allocationLookupTable['Capacity_min']
<=  riskCapacityScore) & (allocationLookupTable['Capacity_max']
>=  riskCapacityScore)
      portfolioID = allocationLookupTable['Portfolio'][(matchTol
& matchCap)]
      return portfolioID.values[0]
```

Compared to the previous class methods, this time, we're using the `@staticmethod` declaration to indicate this method is not dependent on any given instance of the `Portfolio` class. This makes sense when you have certain helper methods that are specific to a class of objects but are independent of any individual variable object of that class. Using some more DataFrame wizardry, we can match the tolerance and capacity scores to end up with a singular portfolio number. Let's see this in practice:

```
riskTolScore = toleranceQuestionnaire.score
riskCapScore = capacityQuestionnaire.score


myPortfolioID = Portfolio.getPortfolioMapping(riskTolScore,
riskCapScore)
print(myPortfolioID)
```

If we reuse the `RiskQuestionnaire` class from *Chapter 7*, and store the result of `calculateScore` in an internal class variable score, then we can directly connect our blocks of code. Obviously, depending on how you answered the questions, you might get a different portfolio even with our example code. So, the output would be a number between 1 and 5, which is now your portfolio.

Now we have technically assembled the beating heart of a Robo-advisor, which is making an investment decision by combining code from the past three chapters. Now, we should elaborate further on two key scenarios in which that decision might be made.

Understanding the differences between self-directed and managed portfolios

The quintessential Robo-advisor journey is one whereby the platform advises the investor on a choice of portfolio, through the proxy of one or more risk questionnaires. These are typically referred to as **managed portfolios**. The keyword here, however, is *advises*. The exact definition will depend on the country, but in most countries, advice implies more stringent regulation and, often, licensing with significant implications. This isn't to be taken lightly, as there could be regulatory, legal, operational, or commercial reasons why, ultimately, you are unable to launch such a platform.

The alternatives to managed portfolios are called **self-directed portfolios**. This is a legal definition that implies the investor is making an explicit choice of portfolio without any explicit advice from the platform. Looking back at our implementation thus far, a self-directed platform would likely omit this last step of risk mapping. In place of this, the investor would have some degree of choice. This might be a slider of how much risk the investor is willing to take for their portfolio, with each notch corresponding to a risk bucket and portfolio. Whether this decision is limited by a risk questionnaire would depend on local regulations.

At the end of the day, it is your job to figure out what the local regulations are and which approach makes more sense for your Robo-advisor with guidance from local legal representation and regulatory approval. It would be wise to seek this information before building a platform, to avoid costly rework down the line.

This concludes our hands-on exploration of creating portfolios. These skills and capabilities will come in handy in the next few chapters as we make good use of our portfolios.

Summary

This chapter has added one of the most important capabilities of our Robo-advisor in constructing our model portfolios. We built up our features starting from very basic properties. We created some simple pie charts to break down the makeup of our example portfolio.

Most of our time and effort was spent on setting up portfolios to match multiple risk bands, using the efficient frontier as our guide. This required several reusable methods to be added to our arsenal, starting from downloading market data from Yahoo Finance.

We ended the chapter by connecting our work with the previous chapter. This mapped our risk tolerance and risk capacity scores to our risk bands, which yields our choice of portfolio. Now we've gone from creating portfolios to connecting them to our risk score from the previous chapter.

In the next chapter, we will evaluate our portfolios in terms of their performance potential, and put together everything we've built so far in completing a Goal-based investment plan.

Further reading

You might be interested in reading some extra information related to the topics discussed in this chapter. Here are a few links to some of the external resources:

- Yan, Yuxing. *Python for Finance, Second Edition.* Packt, 2017: `https://www.packtpub.com/product/python-for-finance-second-edition/9781787125698.`

- Charles Schwab. *Investor Profile Questionnaire.* Accessed online 21.10.2022: `https://www.schwab.com/resource/investment-questionnaire`

9
Investment Projections

This chapter will build on what we have just completed with portfolios. Probably the most interesting question about any portfolio is performance, or how much money it will return against your initial investment. When evaluating portfolios, we often project past performance into the future as a guideline of what to expect. As everyone knows, past performance does not guarantee future returns, but at least you'll have some idea of the relative risk and reward of the portfolio.

In this chapter, we will look at some key concepts required to make basic calculations for the future value of our investments. From there, we will start building some code for calculating and visualizing projections in different ways. Finally, we will tie these together with previous chapters to look at a complete Goal-based investment plan and evaluate **Goal probability**. By the end of the chapter, you'll have learned how to create investment projections in Python, and how to visualize projections for your portfolios.

In this chapter, we're going to cover the following topics:

- Learning about key inputs for calculating projections
- Calculating investment projections
- Visualizing investment projections
- Calculating Goal probability

Learning about key inputs for calculating projections

Before we start writing more code, we will cover a few basic terms and formulas that will come in handy in this chapter:

- **Future Value**: This is how we calculate the value of our investment in the future, based on the interest rate and investment period:

$$FV = PV \times (1 + r)^n$$

Where:

- *FV* is the future value
- *PV* is the present value
- *r* is the interest rate
- *n* is the number of periods

- **Compound Interest**: Whenever you apply an interest rate repeatedly, you end up compounding the interest. There is a slight change from the FV formula:

$$FV = PV \times \left(1 + \frac{r}{n}\right)^{(n \times t)}$$

Where:

- *FV* is the future value
- *PV* is the present value
- *r* is the interest rate
- *n* is the number of periods
- *t* is the number of years

- **Annuity**: If we wish to make regular deposits, we will need to calculate an annuity as well. An annuity is effectively compound interest but with regular contributions. The formula is as follows.

$$FVA = PMT \times \frac{\left(1 + \frac{r}{n}\right)^{(n \times t)} - 1}{\frac{r}{n}}$$

Where:

- *FVA* is the future value of the annuity
- *PMT* is the recurring deposit
- *r* is the interest rate
- *n* is the number of periods
- *t* is the number of years

We will immediately make good use of these formulas, starting with future value.

Calculating investment projections

Let's start from the basics using some simple assumptions to calculate how interest will increase our investment value over 1 year:

```
expectedReturn = 0.08
initialInvestment = 5000
years = 1
valuePrincipal = initialInvestment * (1 + expectedReturn)
print(valuePrincipal)
```

In this example, I used an 8% expected return for my portfolio and an initial investment of 5,000. So the result would be 5,400 if the interest from our portfolio return is applied at the end of the year. If we generalized this formula for monthly interest instead, we would get the following:

```
valuePrincipal = initialInvestment * pow(1 + expectedReturn/12,
(years*12))
print(valuePrincipal)
```

Here, we make use of the pow function to implement the power used in the original formula. Due to the more frequent compounding, the result would be slightly higher at 5414.99. If we were to allow only one-time investments into our portfolios, this would be all we need. In reality, that would be extremely limiting in terms of enabling investors to reach their Goals and your platform to accumulate assets and revenues from fees. Therefore, we would want to calculate the value based on monthly deposits:

```
monthlyInvestment = 100
valueMonthly = monthlyInvestment * (pow(1 + expectedReturn/12,
(years*12))-1)/(expectedReturn/12)
print(valueMonthly)
```

In this case, you will see 1244.99. Of course, this formula is still missing the initial investment, so we need to combine the two to get what we need. This will give investors the flexibility to invest zero or more as initial and monthly deposits:

```
totalValue = valuePrincipal + valueMonthly
print(totalValue)
```

In this case, you will get the output as 6659.99. If we put this together into a reusable method, it would look like this:

```
def returnProjection(expectedReturn, initialInvestment,
monthlyInvestment, years):
```

```
    valuePrincipal = initialInvestment * pow(1 +
expectedReturn/12, (years*12))
    valueMonthly = monthlyInvestment * (pow(1 +
expectedReturn/12, (years*12))-1)/(expectedReturn/12)
    return valuePrincipal+valueMonthly
```

This is all well and good if we always get the return that we expect. But in reality, this is almost never the case. Remember what we've learned about MPT—expected returns come with expected risk. This risk represents volatility, which can go either way—up or down. This is why we need to carefully model portfolios and measure investors' risk appetite. So, the next logical step is to add expected risk to our projections. Typically, we would look at two scenarios: one standard deviation above and below the average return.

> **Note**
>
> When using the PyPortfolioOpt module, the Volatility property returned by portfolio_performance() is already the standard deviation of variance.

Let's add our expected risk:

```
expectedRisk = 0.10
expectedReturnMin = expectedReturn - expectedRisk
expectedReturnMax = expectedReturn + expectedRisk
print(expectedReturnMin)
print(returnProjection(expectedReturnMin, initialInvestment,
monthlyInvestment, years))
print(expectedReturnMax)
print(returnProjection(expectedReturnMax, initialInvestment,
monthlyInvestment, years))
```

In this case, we've assumed an expected risk of 10% for our portfolio. Let's see the output:

```
-0.020000000000000004
6089.97247567486
0.18
7282.212000384563
```

This means that the worst performance we should expect would be -2% per year, and the best a whopping 18%. The corresponding range of one-year performance would be between 6089 and 7282. From here, we can move on to visualizing performance over time.

Visualizing investment projections

The first thing we're going to need is the ability to calculate the preceding projections year by year, so we can eventually plot the outcome. Let's see how we can do that:

```python
def returnProjectionByYear(expectedReturn, expectedRisk,
initialInvestment, monthlyInvestment, years):
    from datetime import date
    import pandas as pd
    df = pd.DataFrame({'date': [],
                       'lowValue': [],
                       'value': [],
                       'highValue': []})
    df.set_index('date')
    for year in range(years+1):
        newValue = returnProjection(expectedReturn,
            initialInvestment,monthlyInvestment, year)
        newValueLower = returnProjection(
            expectedReturn-expectedRisk,
            initialInvestment, monthlyInvestment, year)
        newValueUpper = returnProjection(
            expectedReturn+expectedRisk,
            initialInvestment, monthlyInvestment, year)
        newDate = date.today()
        newDate = newDate.replace(year=newDate.year + year)
        df = df.append(pd.Series({'date': newDate,
            'lowValue': newValueLower, 'value': newValue,
            'highValue': newValueUpper}, name=''))
    df = df.set_index(pd.DatetimeIndex(df['date']))
    df = df.drop(columns="date")
    return df
```

In this method, we will build a new DataFrame table from scratch, and then add values for each year in a loop. Lastly, we add an index column based on the date. Let's try this with the data from our previous example:

```python
data = returnProjectionByYear(expectedReturn, expectedRisk,
initialInvestment, monthlyInvestment, years)
data
```

We'll get the following output:

date	lowValue	value	highValue
2022-10-23	5000.000000	5000.000000	5000.000
2023-10-23	6089.972476	6659.990136	7282.212

Figure 9.1 – Example output from year-by-year projections

The good thing is we can see the values still match our previous work; so the method is doing what we intended. Let's look at a more useful example that stretches this out some years further. All we need to do is change the years variable to 10, which would yield this:

date	lowValue	value	highValue
2022-10-23	5000.000000	5000.000000	5000.000000
2023-10-23	6089.972476	6659.990136	7282.212000
2024-10-23	7158.344224	8457.758635	10010.866139
2025-10-23	8205.543322	10404.741032	13273.294611
2026-10-23	9231.989361	12513.322009	17173.913375
2027-10-23	10238.093620	14796.914166	21837.564050
2028-10-23	11224.259225	17270.043346	27413.509541
2029-10-23	12190.881315	19948.441029	34080.211294
2030-10-23	13138.347196	22849.144398	42051.041054
2031-10-23	14067.036500	25990.604716	51581.109956
2032-10-23	14977.321335	29392.804691	62975.433510

Figure 9.2 – The same example for 10 years

This gives us something worth visualizing. So, let's do exactly that with a simple chart:

```
import matplotlib.pyplot as plt
plt.plot(data.index, data['highValue'], label="High")
plt.plot(data.index, data['value'], label="Expected")
plt.plot(data.index, data['lowValue'], label="Low")
```

```
plt.legend(loc="upper left")
plt.show()
```

This will generate the following output:

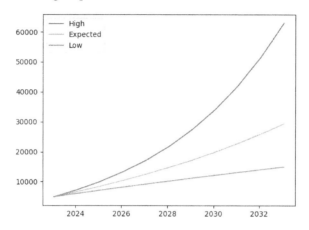

Figure 9.3 – Example visualization of 10 years of performance data

This immediately highlights the value of compound interest in a way that tables would allow. Not only does a higher return give you more money, but that difference accelerates every year. If you run the same exercise for 30 years, it will be quite striking.

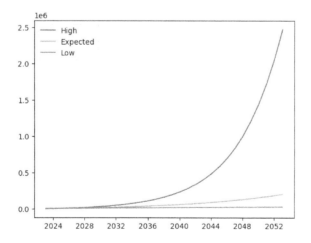

Figure 9.4 – Example visualization of 30 years of performance data

At this point, it's worthwhile remembering that the green line represents the maximum return line. In reality, you will not follow any of these lines exactly over 30 years. This just establishes the range of possibilities and the upper and bottom ranges of likely portfolio movements.

Stochastic methods such as **Monte Carlo** can be used to generate more realistic paths over time. While it isn't that popular with Robo-advisors, it is quite commonly used in other investment applications. Luckily, as with most things, we can just use a Python library to quickly test this out. If you did want to build your own Monte Carlo projection method, it isn't that hard as we're just taking random walks using the average return and standard deviation. Let's give it a shot and install `pandas_montecarlo`:

```
!pip install pandas_montecarlo --upgrade --no-cache-dir
```

Now we can try this out easily with a few lines of code on one of our portfolios from before:

```
import pandas_montecarlo
data = yf.download("VTI TLT IEI GLD DBC", group_by="Ticker",
period="20y")
data = data.iloc[:, data.columns.get_level_values(1)=="Close"]
data = data.dropna()
data.columns = data.columns.droplevel(1)
data['Total'] = data.sum(axis=1)
data['Return'] = data['Total'].pct_change().fillna(0)
mc = data['Return'].montecarlo(sims=100)
mc.plot(title="Portfolio Returns Monte Carlo Simulations",
figsize=(12,7))
```

You'll see something like this:

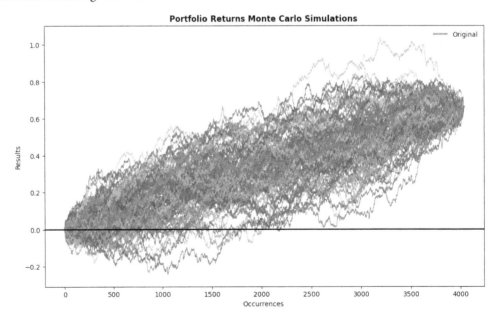

Figure 9.5 – Example Monte Carlo simulation

While this is quite visually interesting, it's just sampling potential random walk paths from our historical data. One positive highlight from such a simulation is that there are generally very few chances to lose money over a time period lasting several decades. For now, let's leave Monte Carlo and get back to where we left off. Now, let's put what we've learned into another class we can reuse easily:

```python
class Projection:
  def __init__(self, expectedReturn: float, expectedRisk:
    float, initialInvestment: float, monthlyInvestment: float,
      years: int):
    from datetime import date
    import pandas as pd
    df = pd.DataFrame({'date': [], 'lowValue': [],
      'value': [], 'highValue': []})
    df.set_index('date')

    for year in range(years+1):
      newValue = self.returnProjection(expectedReturn,
          initialInvestment, monthlyInvestment, year)
      newValueLower = self.returnProjection(
        expectedReturn-expectedRisk, initialInvestment,
        monthlyInvestment, year)
      newValueUpper = self.returnProjection(
          expectedReturn+expectedRisk, initialInvestment,
          monthlyInvestment, year)
      newDate = date.today()
      newDate = newDate.replace(year=newDate.year + year)
      df = df.append(pd.Series({'date': newDate,
        'lowValue': newValueLower, 'value': newValue,
        'highValue': newValueUpper},name=''))

    df = df.set_index(pd.DatetimeIndex(df['date']))
    df = df.drop(columns="date")
    self.data = df
```

Now let's complete the class by adding a few useful helper functions as class methods:

```python
  @staticmethod
  def returnProjection(expectedReturn, initialInvestment,
```

```
    monthlyInvestment, years):
    valuePrincipal = initialInvestment * pow(
        1 + expectedReturn/12, (years*12))
    valueMonthly = monthlyInvestment * (pow(
        1 + expectedReturn/12, (
        years*12))-1)/expectedReturn/12)
    return valuePrincipal+valueMonthly

  def visualize(self, targetAmount: float = 0.0):
    import matplotlib.pyplot as plt
    import matplotlib.ticker as ticker
    scale_y = 1e6
    ticks_y = ticker.FuncFormatter(lambda x, pos: '{
        0:g}'.format(x/scale_y))
    fig, ax=plt.subplots()
    ax.yaxis.set_major_formatter(ticks_y)
    ax.set_ylabel('Millions (USD)')
    ax.plot(self.data.index, self.data['value'])
    ax.plot(self.data.index, self.data['lowValue'])
    ax.plot(self.data.index, self.data['highValue'])
    if (targetAmount > 0):
      plt.axhline(y=targetAmount)
    plt.show()
```

The only new functionality we've added is the optional ability to add a horizontal line to indicate a Goal target amount. We'll make good use of that next. Let's connect more of our Robo-advisor building blocks now, by combining capabilities and classes we've built for Goals, risk questionnaires, portfolios, and projections:

1.   Let's first create a Goal:

```
    myGoal = Goal("Retirement",
                  targetYear=2041,
                  targetValue=3000000,
                  initialContribution=50000,
                  monthlyContribution=500,
                  priority="Wishes")
```

2. Let's fill in a risk questionnaire:

```
questionsFileName = '/content/Data/Risk Questions.csv'
answersFileName = '/content/Data/Risk Answers.csv'

toleranceQuestionnaire = RiskQuestionnaire()
toleranceQuestionnaire.
loadQuestionnaire(questionsFileName, answersFileName,
"Tolerance")

capacityQuestionnaire = RiskQuestionnaire()
capacityQuestionnaire.loadQuestionnaire(questionsFileName,
answersFileName, "Capacity")

toleranceQuestionnaire.answerQuestionnaire()
capacityQuestionnaire.answerQuestionnaire()
```

3. Let's calculate our risk scores:

```
toleranceQuestionnaire.calculateScore()
capacityQuestionnaire.calculateScore()
riskTolScore = toleranceQuestionnaire.score
riskCapScore = capacityQuestionnaire.score
```

4. Let's generate a portfolio that maps to our risk score:

```
myPortfolioID = Portfolio.
getPortfolioMapping(riskTolScore, riskCapScore)
myPortfolio = Portfolio("VTI TLT IEI GLD DBC",
expectedReturn = 0.06, portfolioName = "Moderate Growth",
riskBucket = myPortfolioID)
```

5. Finally, let's create a projection:

```
from datetime import date
yearsToGoal = myGoal.targetYear - date.today().year
myProjection = Projection(myPortfolio.expectedReturn,
expectedRisk = myPortfolio.expectedRisk,
initialInvestment = myGoal.initialContribution,
monthlyInvestment = myGoal.monthlyContribution,
    years = yearsToGoal)
myProjection.visualize(myGoal.targetValue)
```

You will get an output that will look something like this, depending on when you run the code, which was January 11, 2023 in our case:

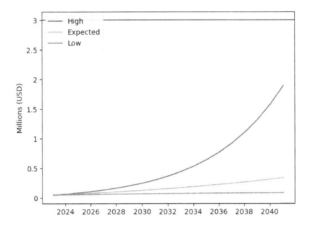

Figure 9.6 – Example projection for our new Goal

Well, what should be visually quite clear is that we're just not going to achieve our Goal. It would be beyond wishful thinking with this plan. So, what can be done about it?

Calculating Goal probability

One way we might evaluate whether our Goal is plausible at all is by just considering the expected return and time horizon. We can use a simple function to compare our Goal target amount to the amount achieved with our expected return at the end of our time horizon:

```
def checkGoalPlausible(df: pd.DataFrame, goalValue) -> bool:
  maxValue = df['value'].max()
  if maxValue >= goalValue:
    return True
  else:
    return False
```

If we run this with our Goal, it should undoubtedly return `False`. While this is a simple heuristic, we would wish to quantify this in more exact terms to know how realistic our Goals are.

We'll now move past simple projections to return to the concept of Goal probability, which we briefly touched on in *Chapter 6*, in the context of Goal priority. These two are naturally connected, as we can use Goal probability to establish a reasonable range for our Goal priority:

```
myGoal.getGoalProbabilities()
```

As we chose the priority as `wishes`, the output would range from 65% to 79%. So, this establishes where we need to be. Now, the question is, what is our Goal probability?

One such method is **Z-Score**, which is a statistical method for estimating the probability of a value falling within a region of the normal distribution. Notice that this is a significant assumption about financial markets. Let's look at the formula and add it to our code:

$$Z = \frac{x - \mu}{\frac{\sigma}{\sqrt{n}}}$$

Where:

- Z is our Z-Score

- x is our sample return

- μ is our average return

- σ is our risk as a standard deviation

- n is our time horizon

Now let's implement this in code:

```
def goalProbability(minReturn, avgReturn, avgRisk, timeHorizon)
-> float:
    import scipy.stats as st
    std = avgRisk/math.sqrt(timeHorizon)
    z_score = (minReturn-avgReturn)/std
    return 1-st.norm.cdf(z_score)
```

We make use of the `scipy.stats` module, which allows us to calculate the probability of our returns being at least that of `minReturn`. Of course, the problem in our case is we don't know what minimum return is needed to reach our target Goal amount. So, we'll need to find it algorithmically, like this:

```
def goalProbabilityForAmount(goalAmount, expectedReturn,
portfolioRisk, years, initialInvestment, monthlyInvestment) ->
float:
    import scipy.stats as st
    import math as math
    std = portfolioRisk/math.sqrt(years)
    amount = 0
    minReturn = 0.00
    while (amount < goalAmount):
```

```
    minReturn = minReturn + 0.0000001
    amount = Projection.returnProjection(minReturn,
        initialInvestment, monthlyInvestment, years)
  z_score = (minReturn-expectedReturn)/std
  return 1-st.norm.cdf(z_score)
```

We're still using the same formula, but now we start from a minimum return of 0.0% and slowly increase until we can reach our target Goal amount. Let's try this:

```
goalProbabilityForAmount(myGoal.targetValue,
                         myPortfolio.expectedReturn,
                         myPortfolio.expectedRisk,
                         yearsToGoal,
                         myGoal.initialContribution,
                         myGoal.monthlyContribution)
```

As expected, this will return quite a sad result, which is very close to zero:

```
1.6038788164252082e-07
```

So, we must figure out how to change our plan. If we cannot increase our risk from the risk questionnaire or portfolio, then we can only change the Goal parameters. Here are the options:

- Wait longer, which would help by allowing more time to accumulate compound interest
- Decrease the target Goal amount, which would lower the bar in our projection and make it easier to achieve
- Increase the initial contribution
- Increase the monthly contribution

Of course, we may need to combine elements of all of these if we are so far off. Often, the monthly contribution is a good place to start. If we fix the other parameters, we can shuffle around the future value formula for a given target amount, and find what monthly contribution is needed:

```
def calculateMonthlyMinimum(expectedReturn, initialInvestment,
years, goalAmount) -> float:
  monthlyInvestment = (goalAmount - (initialInvestment * pow(
    1 + expectedReturn/12, (years*12))))/((pow(
    1 + expectedReturn/12, (years*12))-1)/(expectedReturn/12))
  return monthlyInvestment
```

Let's try this out:

```
calculateMonthlyMinimum(myPortfolio.expectedReturn,
                        myGoal.initialContribution,
                        yearsToGoal,
                        myGoal.targetValue)
```

This will yield a rather steep $6,714.45 per month. For the sake of the exercise, let's do that update and see what we get now:

```
myGoal.monthlyContribution =
calculateMonthlyMinimum(myPortfolio.expectedReturn, myGoal.
initialContribution, yearsToGoal, myGoal.targetValue)

goalProbabilityForAmount(myGoal.targetValue,
                         myPortfolio.expectedReturn,
                         myPortfolio.expectedRisk,
                         yearsToGoal,
                         myGoal.initialContribution,
                         myGoal.monthlyContribution)
```

This gets us into the ballpark now with 50%, which means we are exactly in the middle of the normal distribution, as one might expect using the expected return rate. There's still a way to go if we want to reach 65% or higher. Let's see what this looks like now:

```
myProjection = Projection(myPortfolio.expectedReturn,
                          myPortfolio.expectedRisk,
                          myGoal.initialContribution,
                          myGoal.monthlyContribution,
                          yearsToGoal)
myProjection.visualize(myGoal.targetValue)
```

From the following output, we can see that now our lines overlap – the Goal amount and expected return collide right on the time horizon.

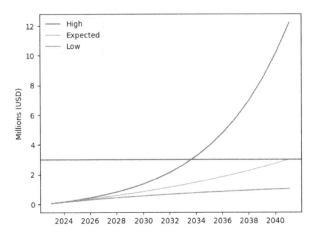

Figure 9.7 – Updated projection with a much higher monthly contribution

From here, we can experiment by extending our time horizon slightly, by imagining a retirement delayed by another 2 years:

```
goalProbabilityForAmount(myGoal.targetValue,
                         myPortfolio.expectedReturn,
                         myPortfolio.expectedRisk,
                         yearsToGoal+2,
                         myGoal.initialContribution,
                         myGoal.monthlyContribution)
```

This should give us above 70%, which is just above our minimum range for our Goal priority. We can visualize this:

```
myProjection = Projection(myPortfolio.expectedReturn,
                          myPortfolio.expectedRisk,
                          myGoal.initialContribution,
                          myGoal.monthlyContribution,
                          yearsToGoal+2)
myProjection.visualize(myGoal.targetValue)
```

This is what you should see:

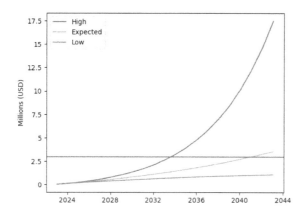

Figure 9.8 – Our target Goal amount finally seems obtainable

We now see the expected return line peeking above our target Goal level, which is what we would expect for a Goal probability above 50%. While we got our result with trial and error in this instance, we can combine several such helper functions to see which levers can be pulled to achieve the desired target probability.

Of course, it is possible that we are taking unnecessary risks in certain cases if the Goal probability is above the range set by the Goal priority. Following is a screenshot from Bambu's Healthcheck API, which offers exactly such a capability. Investors can simply click from the menu to fix their Goal in the way that seems most reasonable to them.

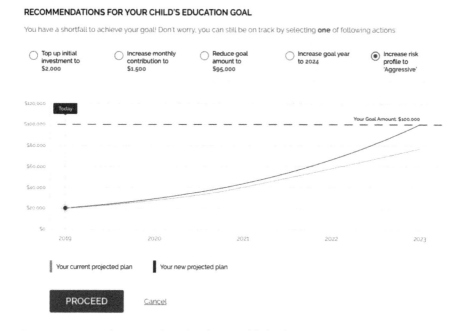

Figure 9.9 – Example actions from Bambu's Healthcheck API to increase Goal probability

> **Note**
>
> In our implementation, we didn't take into consideration certain items, such as fees and taxes, which will impact investment performance over time.

We've now gathered all the capabilities we need to make investments and financial plans with our Robo-advisor, so it's time to start moving some money by looking at account opening in the next chapter.

Summary

This chapter concludes our core capabilities for creating an investment plan with our Robo-advisor. We started by looking at some basic calculations for projecting how our investments might appreciate in the future. From there, we combined several formulas to come up with a reusable method that accounts for ongoing monthly deposits.

We moved on to visualizing our projections to communicate potential investment outcomes. Then we put together all our core capabilities from earlier chapters to create a new Goal, answer risk tolerance and risk capacity questions, create a model portfolio, and map our risk score to a model portfolio.

With our new Goal, we looked at ways to estimate the probability of achieving our target Goal amount in our planned time horizon. Finally, we built some additional methods to help us calculate Goal probability and find appropriate financial parameters for us to achieve our Goal.

By the end of the chapter, you will have learned hands-on how to create projections and visualizations for your portfolios and related Goals. In terms of our overall workflow, this chapter marks our transition from financial planning to the practical implementation of our investment plan, which starts with opening an account. In the next chapter, we will look at various prerequisites for opening accounts and various types of accounts to hold our cash and investments.

10
Account Opening and KYC

In this chapter, we will move from investment capabilities to operational capabilities. We will learn about the typical information required by Robo-advisors and custodians for opening accounts. As part of that process, we will learn about some techniques for validating information provided by investors. We will also try to digitally sign documents hands-on and use some **artificial intelligence** (**AI**) to read identity documents uploaded by investors. Finally, we will look at an overall **know your customer** (**KYC**) process and try some **anti-money laundering** (**AML**) checks hands-on.

In this chapter, we're going to cover the following topics:

- Learning about the typical information required to open investment accounts
- Understand the KYC workflow

Learning about the typical information required to open investment accounts

With most Robo-advisors, you will be required to create a user account before you can access any other features, including those from previous chapters. Typically, that may only necessitate sharing an email address and creating a password. This email address may be validated with a one-time code to ensure it is valid, as fake email addresses would be a problem for a financially regulated platform.

By the time you reach the actual account opening phase, we are talking about opening a custodial account at the custodian, not a user in your Robo-advisor database. You will need to link the two once the account has been created. What type of information is needed from the investor is going to be largely dictated by the custodian. The information will be sent to the custodian either via batch file transfer or an API if they offer it.

> **Note**
> Before you can access such account-opening APIs, you will need to register your company and platform with the custodian and get approval for the Robo-advisor you are building. This may often involve the upfront costs of opening master accounts and depositing minimum balances.

For the sake of this exercise, let's assume you've taken care of all that, and the task at hand is now gathering the necessary information from your investors. Here's some typical data you would be collecting.

Basic information for KYC

The terms –KYC and AML, are industry terms used to refer to specific legislation around verifying the identity and suitability of customers and partners. These are specific rules and laws defined by local law and financial regulations.

Here are some typical fields you may encounter in an account opening form for a Robo-advisor. This isn't complete or exhaustive and will vary by country and choice of custodian and is subject to change with regulations:

- **Prefix(es), Given Name, Additional Name(s), Family Name, Suffix(es), Legal Name(s)**: This is just basic information expected to identify you for KYC and AML purposes.

- **Country of citizenship, Country of birth, Country of residence, Residency/visa status**: Basic KYC and AML information. Depending on your answer, you may be considered ineligible. For example, most US Robo-advisors do not allow foreign investors without a US address or **Social Security Number** (**SSN**) to open accounts.

- **Date of birth, Social Security Number, Tax Number**: This is primarily used to confirm identification.

- **Marital status, Number of dependents**: Basic KYC information.

- **Phone Number, Email address**: Basic KYC information.

- **Street address, City, State, Postal code, Country**: Basic KYC and AML information.

- **Employment status, Employer, Position, Years Employed**: Basic KYC and AML information. This could be latest or previous, years of experience, and employers.

- **Source of funds, political person status**: This is key AML information and may come with specific definitions of what answers are allowed or a simple multiple choice.

While the preceding information seems quite simple, in reality, custodians will be very exact in the format of data they are willing to process. This puts a large emphasis on data validation. Let's look at a few examples.

Data validation examples

Data validation just means that we check the format of the investor's data input and advise them on the correct format where validation errors occur. We used such validation errors in some of our algorithms in previous chapters. Now, instead of a simple comparison of equal values, we will need something more sophisticated:

```
import re
user_name = input("Please enter your Family Name: ")
if not re.match("^[\w' -]*$", user_name):
    print ("Error! Make sure you only use alphanumerics and the
characters dash, space, and apostrophe in your name")
```

Here, we make use of something called **regular expressions** (**regexes**), which are commonly used to match strings with a set of pre-defined rules. You can use free tools such as https://regex101.com/ to build and test your rules. In our example, we are forming a one-line response that can include any number of word characters (\w), as well as characters for dashes, spaces, and apostrophes. A slight variation of this might be to only allow letters, not numbers, and limit the response to between 1 and 64 characters, which might be a limitation set by the custodian:

```
user_name = input("Please enter your Family Name: ")
if not re.match("^[a-zA-Z' -]{1,64}$", user_name):
    print ("Error! Make sure you only use letters and the
characters dash, space, and apostrophe in your name")
```

Here, we can see the ranges of a-zA-Z denoting the alphabet and {1,64} replacing the star character to denote possible lengths. For other fields, such as an SSN or phone number, we can have more rigid rules in place:

```
phone_no = input("Please enter your Phone Number: ")
if not re.match("\d\d\d-\d\d\d-\d\d\d\d", phone_no):
    print ("Error! Please ensure your phone number follows the
format 123-456-7890.")
```

Here, we denote the individual characters one by one, with \d being a single digit. Here's an example of an SSN validation:

```
ssn_no = input("Please enter your SSN: ")
if not re.match("^(?!(000|666|9))\d{3}-(?!00)\d{2}-
(?!0000)\d{4}$", ssn_no):
    print ("Error! Please check your SSN.")
```

Here, we have a general format of three digits, a dash, two digits, a dash, and four digits. The additional rules are that it can't start with a 9, the first section can't be 000 or 666, and the second and third sections can't be all 0s. Such rules are country-specific, and you should check with your custodian to match your rules.

Certain fields, such as addresses, are typically beyond your standard regex ruleset and would benefit from an API to check whether the address is real. In many countries, postal services offer free APIs that you can seek out for this purpose. For the sake of convenience, we will take a look at a paid API that has a dedicated Python module called `smartystreets`. We can install it using the familiar `pip install` command, as follows:

```
pip install smartystreets_python_sdk
```

Here's some sample code provided with the module, to test it out. Do note that to run this code, you will need to at least sign up for their free trial, which includes up to 1,000 calls of this API:

```
from smartystreets_python_sdk import StaticCredentials,
ClientBuilder
from smartystreets_python_sdk.us_street import Lookup

auth_id = "your_id"
auth_token = "your_token"
credentials = StaticCredentials(auth_id, auth_token)
print("Step 0. Wire up the client with your keypair.")
client = ClientBuilder(credentials).build_us_street_api_
client()
print("Step 1. Make a lookup. (BTW, you can also send entire
batches of lookups...)")
lookup = Lookup()
lookup.street = "1 Rosedale"
lookup.lastline = "Baltimore MD"
lookup.candidates = 10

print("Step 2. Send the lookup.")
client.send_lookup(lookup)

print("Step 3. Show the resulting candidate addresses:")
for c, candidate in enumerate(lookup.result):
    print("- {}: {}, {}".format(c, candidate.delivery_line_1,
candidate.last_line))
```

This example tries to match a partial address with no postcode included and will return up to 10 potential addresses that match this information. Again, the preceding code will return an authentication error unless you add your credentials at the top.

Now, let's upload some documents needed for KYC.

Documents for KYC

In a typical Robo-advisor, for KYC, you will see that at least two key documents are needed from all new investors: a Terms of Service document, and some type of investor disclaimer. Again, these would be highly dependent on the custodian and the country in question. Often, these documents are pre-populated from the KYC information provided by the investor, and just require a digital signature to be added.

The other category of documentation required is for KYC itself, to confirm your identity. This might include uploading a scanned copy of your passport or other local identification such as a driver's license. Furthermore, many custodians will need to see proof of address, which is typically a utility bill of some sort or an official bank statement. Some methods of character recognition or text extraction may be used to facilitate the review, but generally, someone needs to look at these documents.

Let's look at some examples that might be useful.

Document upload example

While we won't get into too much depth into digital forms and signatures, let's look at a brief example using the free pyHanko module. In reality, when building your Robo-advisor as a platform, you will likely be using some type of digital document service such as Docusign to handle all this. Remember, your solutions must comply with the custodian's requirements for documents, as well as local regulations. Once you have used pip to install pyHanko, you can try something like the following:

```
!pip install nest_asyncio
import nest_asyncio
nest_asyncio.apply()
from pyhanko.sign import signers
from pyhanko.pdf_utils.incremental_writer import
IncrementalPdfFileWriter


cms_signer = signers.SimpleSigner.load(
    'key.pem', 'cert.pem',
    key_passphrase=b'yourpassword'
)
```

```
with open('document.pdf', 'r+b') as doc:
    w = IncrementalPdfFileWriter(doc)
    out = signers.sign_pdf(
        w, signers.PdfSignatureMetadata(
            field_name='Signature1'),
        signer=cms_signer,
        in_place=False
    )


with open("signed.pdf", "wb") as f:
    f.write(out.getbuffer())
```

If you rename and upload any PDF file to Colab as document.pdf, the code will produce a document with an invisible cryptographic signature to prove its authenticity. The same signature can also be validated using PyHanko or any other software including Adobe. PyHanko does support visible signature stamps as shown in the following screenshot, but we will leave that to you to experiment if relevant:

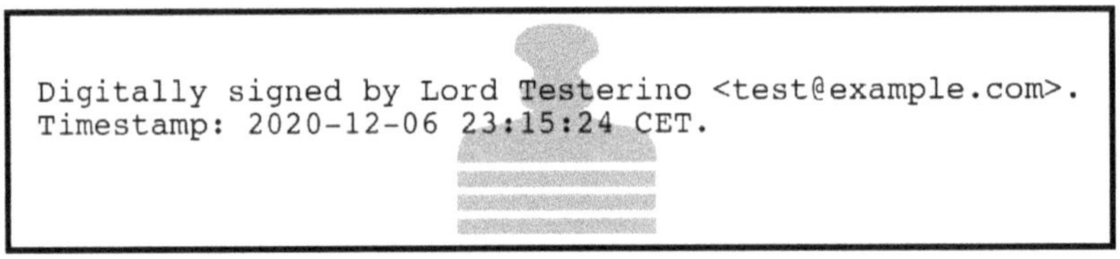

Figure 10.1 – Example digital signature from pyHanko

If you don't already have a private key and certificate file, you'll need to generate them first. You can do that directly on Colab as follows:

```
!openssl req -x509 -newkey rsa:4096 -keyout key.pem -out cert.
pem -sha256 -days 365
```

This will give you private keys and private certificate files and you can see them in your Colab folder. and can now be used with PyHanko. Note that, this means that Adobe or other PDF readers will show a warning that this certificate is not from a trusted authority. If you do need a third party trusted certificate, which you would for a commercial use case, you can purchase one online from providers such as SSL at https://www.ssl.com/certificates/document-signing-certificates/. In this case, all you need is to generate a private key of your own, the certificate would come from the authority.

```
!openssl genpkey -algorithm RSA -out key.pem
```

This will generate a new private key file in your Colab folder.

Let's now look at some other useful tools we can try.

Document data extraction

Another useful thing we can do is try data extraction from a passport. Again, there is a multitude of paid APIs you could try, but there's a free Python module called `PassportEye`. In this case, its installation is slightly more involved, so let's follow the instructions specifically for Google Colab:

```
!pip install PassportEye
!apt install tesseract-ocr
!pip install pytesseract
```

Once these commands have been run successfully, you need to do one more thing to get everything to work. This is to make sure that the `pytesseract` commands within the module work correctly:

```
import pytesseract
pytesseract.pytesseract.tesseract_cmd = r'/usr/bin/tesseract'
```

Now, we can use the module, with just one line:

```
from passporteye import read_mrz
mrz = read_mrz('/content/drive/MyDrive/Books/Robo-advisor with
Python/Data/passport-td3.png')
```

I took the example file from the module home page on GitHub (`https://github.com/konstantint/PassportEye/tree/master/tests/data`). You can do the same and upload the image to your Colab. This is what it looks like:

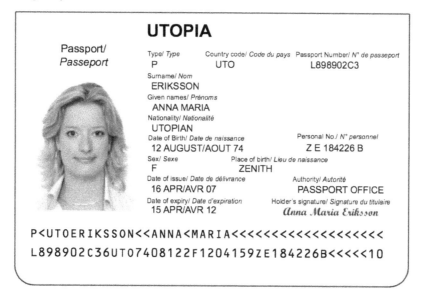

Figure 10.2 – Example fake test passport from PassportEye

Now, to examine what we got from our attempt at reading this image file, we will run `print` `(mrz.number)`, which returns **L898902C3**. That's pretty cool, isn't it? Beneath these Python modules are some real smarts, and interesting history, too. It was one of the original **Optical Character Recognition** (**OCR**) algorithms developed by Hewlett-Packard in the 1980s, and is now open source and maintained by Google. Over the years, it has become more advanced and now supports neural networks with long short-term memory layers. At least now you can claim your Robo-advisor has some AI included!

Moving on, let's put all this information together and look at what the KYC workflow might look like.

Understanding the KYC workflow

We've already gathered basic data from the investor, added digital signatures, and even extracted passport information using some AI magic. To look at the big picture, the overall flow of account opening will be dependent on your custodian. If they just expect a whole pile of files to be sent via batch transfer, then the flow is mostly yours to decide. However, most will support APIs that would likely require a specific sequence of calls to get an account approved.

Here are some basic steps to expect in a KYC workflow:

1. The investor registers an account

2. The investor enters basic KYC and AML information

3. The investor uploads proof of identity and proof of address

4. The investor completes and signs the documentation

5. Compliance review of items

6. Compliance performs AML checks

7. Compliance sends additional information requests (optional)

8. Investor submits additional information (optional)

9. Account approval (or rejection)

10. The account is opened for funding and investments

During this process, one key piece of information to keep track of is the account status, which indicates the stage of approval the custodian has registered for the account. The exact states would depend on the custodian, but you can expect indications of identity verification, document upload, document verification, and such to be included in codes for account status. This will also help you communicate issues to the investor, for example, if the documents provided did not pass the internal checks of the custodian.

Accounts may also become frozen or suspended at any time even after being approved, for failing various internal rules set by the custodian and regulators. Therefore, this value would be potentially updated every time the investor logged into their account via your Robo-advisor.

This whole process may or may not be done in real time. Often, the various verification steps will take hours or even days to verify, so the investor may only be able to complete one step at a time instead of finishing the entire process.

One key part of the process will be conducting AML checks to confirm that you are indeed allowed to open an account for the investor.

AML checks

Your custodian will be running their own KYC and AML process, but that doesn't mean you shouldn't. One handy tool for this purpose is the **Specially Designated Nationals And Blocked Persons List (SDN)** maintained by the US Department of The Treasury. This is a 2,000-page list of people and businesses you probably don't want as investors on your platform.

Because the list is published and maintained online, we can simply download it into Python, like so:

```
import requests
response = requests.get("https://www.treasury.gov/ofac/
downloads/sdnlist.txt")
data = response.text
```

Now, we have a very large string object in the data variable that we can search in different ways. As a starting point, you would probably check the last name of the investor and see what comes up.

If you run data.find("Ranin"), using my last name, I'm hoping the result will be -1, which indicates no hits. If you run the same with the name Zakharova, you should get some hits with the return value indicating the index inside the file. This already is a reason to investigate further:

```
for item in data.split("\n"):
  if "Zakharova" in item:
    print (item.strip())
```

This piece of code will simply print out any line that contains this name so that we can get a sense of what kind of hits we're getting:

```
AVIA; a.k.a. TRANSAVIAEXPORT AIRLINES), 44, Zakharova Str.,
Minsk
AVIA; a.k.a. TRANSAVIAEXPORT AIRLINES), 44, Zakharova Str.,
Minsk
AVIA; a.k.a. TRANSAVIAEXPORT AIRLINES), 44, Zakharova Str.,
Minsk
AVIA; a.k.a. TRANSAVIAEXPORT AIRLINES), 44, Zakharova Str.,
Minsk
```

```
AVIA; a.k.a. TRANSAVIAEXPORT AIRLINES), 44, Zakharova Str.,
Minsk
AVIA; a.k.a. TRANSAVIAEXPORT AIRLINES), 44, Zakharova Str.,
Minsk
AVIA; a.k.a. TRANSAVIAEXPORT AIRLINES), 44, Zakharova Str.,
Minsk
AVIA; a.k.a. TRANSAVIAEXPORT AIRLINES), 44, Zakharova Str.,
Minsk
Zakharova Str., Minsk 220034, Belarus; d. 11, Ul.
Pervomayskaya,
TRANSAVIAEXPORT AIRLINES), 44, Zakharova Str., Minsk 220034,
TRANSAVIAEKSPORT; a.k.a. TRANSAVIAEXPORT AIRLINES), 44,
Zakharova
a.k.a. OTKRYTOYE AKTSIONERNOYE OBSCHESTVO TAE AVIA), 44,
Zakharova
```

Frankly, if you get any hits at all for last names, aliases, addresses, or company names, you would want to take a look at the PDF version and read it for yourself. If you're getting direct hits, you may want to simply reject the investor on that basis to avoid any liability for yourself. This isn't a comprehensive solution for AML but serves as an example of various free and commercial databases and APIs available for the job.

It's worth noting that it's guaranteed your custodian will perform their own KYC and AML process. This doesn't mean you shouldn't. At the end of the day, as a Robo-advisor, you will be liable for the clients you accept and provide investment advice and/or products to. As these are highly specific to the country in question and the type of investors you are targeting, it is best to consult with local authorities on requirements.

Accounting for Goals

One further complication to factor in is Goals. Most early Robo-advisors only supported one account type and each investor was allocated an investment account. That keeps account opening, reporting, and statements very neat and tidy. Once Goals were introduced, they presented a challenge. Do you lump together multiple Goals into one investment account, split them out so that each Goal has its own account, or introduce some further subaccount structure?

Ultimately, this choice will depend on your custodian and broker – what account types they support, the fee structure for opening and maintaining multiple accounts, and options for virtual accounts or subaccounts. We will return to this topic in *Chapter 12, Order Management and Execution*, once we create some orders.

Special account types

For this book, we will assume the simplest form of investment account with no special features, which is the individual investment account. However, it is worth noting that in many countries, there are a whole host of specialized account types that are designed for different investment scenarios. The obvious one is joint accounts between spouses.

In countries that have taxes on investments or offer government pension plans, there is often a need for some form of retirement account. America has the 401k and **Individual Retirement Account (IRA)**, Australia has Superannuation, and Singapore has the **Central Provident Fund (CPF)**. All of these are local forms of retirement accounts. In practice, the idea is to offer tax incentives for keeping money locked away until retirement, and tax penalties for taking money out early. In many cases, these retirement accounts also have limits on how much money can be contributed over a calendar year or a lifetime, and whether the money comes from the individual and/or employer.

In practice, these special account types will introduce additional fields and/or steps into the workflow. In the case of tax-deferred accounts, one change will be to ensure limits for annual contributions are not exceeded. Because all of this logic is highly specific to each country, we will leave it outside the scope of this book.

There is also the question of structuring accounts between investors. To begin with, you could just have one individual account for each investor, and then trade and report on them individually. In practice, when dealing with large numbers of investors and accounts, it starts to make more sense to aggregate these under one master, or omnibus account. This means all trades are made in one large account, and then allocated back to individual subaccounts. This often makes trading faster and more cost-efficient but does introduce complexities into the implementation and order management in particular. Again, local regulations will determine what is possible and cost-efficient.

We will leave these complexities as they're outside the scope of this book, but it is worth noting that these specialized account types will play an increasingly important role as Robo-advisors expand the scope of services and financial planning tools they provide.

With that, we've tried some hands-on KYC and AML using a variety of helpful Python modules. While this exploration was high-level, we will move on and try out some methods for funding our new accounts.

Summary

This chapter moved our Robo-advisor past the core investment capabilities and on to the operational capabilities needed to enable investors to transact. We looked at the types of data typically required by custodians to open new accounts, starting with basic investor information. We tried a few examples of field validation using regexps.

From there, we looked at various types of documents typically needed for KYC. We tried to sign a test document using a digital cryptographic signature and used some AI to extract information from a sample passport image. We also reviewed the basic steps in a KYC workflow and looked at an example of AML checks. We tried using an online database to check whether our investor or related companies were listed as potentially blacklisted by the American government.

Now that we have an account set up, we can move some imaginary money into our account in preparation for making our first investment transaction.

11

Funding Your Account

In this chapter, we will introduce one last prerequisite for transactions: funding the account we've just created with the custodian. We will look at two different methods of transferring funds – wire transfers and direct debit transfers. Wire transfers are the obvious and easy solution, but they rely on the investor leaving your site and initiating the transfer from their online bank. Generally, the ideal solution is always direct debit, which means the investor experience does not halt between onboarding and funding. The downside with direct debit is that it requires a country-specific integration with a payment gateway provider. We will use the Plaid API to build an example direct debit workflow for the US market that enables an investor to log into their own bank account and choose an amount to transfer to your Robo-advisor account.

By the end of the chapter, you will have gained the knowledge and skills required to implement an account funding mechanism for your Robo-advisor. Some aspects of that implementation may differ depending on your country and available providers, but the principles will be the same.

In this chapter, we're going to cover the following topics:

* Initiating wire transfers
* Initiating direct debit transfers

Initiating wire transfers

If you want to invest money on behalf of your investors, you need to have money from your investors. Therefore, investors will need to move money from their own bank account into their new investment account at your custodian.

By far the simplest way to do that is a **wire transfer**. Fundamentally, all you need to do on the frontend is simply display the wire transfer details of your custodian bank. This would include the recipient's (your Robo-advisor or investor) name, address, bank account number, and routing number (ABA, SWIFT, etc.) where applicable. That's it. In the case of international transfers, this would expand with the receiving bank's SWIFT BIC, IBAN format bank account number, and an international payments system routing code – all of which you would get from your custodian.

The tricky part is that the investor must now leave your Robo-advisor to make this wire transfer, which they may or may not ever do. Furthermore, it will take several days at least to make this transfer and may incur fees for both parties in doing so. Let's look at what it would take to confirm the transfer has been completed.

Validating wire transfers

Given that the integration to your custodian is going to be fully dependent on your choice of a local provider, we are generally bypassing that considerable effort, as it's beyond the scope of this book. When we talk about transferring money though, it is important to consider how your Robo-advisor will get access to those funds. In the previous chapter, we talked about opening accounts. So, at this point, we can assume the customer has at least one account number registered with the custodian.

If the custodian has an API to open accounts, you would have already received a number as an API response. Alternatively, accounts may be updated via a **start of day** (**SOD**) file. You can access these files through a secure **File Transfer Protocol** (**FTP**) site. These files are again specific to custodians, but would typically include information about clients, accounts, cash movements, and open positions in investment products. They are typically formatted as **comma-separated value** (**CSV**) files and can seem very cryptic to the naked eye, containing a myriad of curious-looking code symbols. Reading these files into your Robo-advisor will require implementing various rules (hopefully, well documented by the custodian) and submitting your platform to a review process before being allowed to transact with live money.

From the perspective of the investor and Robo-advisor, by far the preferred method of funding an account is direct debit. Let's look at this in more detail. If you're building a Robo-advisor for your own usage, then you can fund your account by wire transfer and move on to the next chapter already.

Initiating direct debit transfers

If initiating a wire transfer is as simple as showing the investor some static text, then a direct debit is the exact opposite. Full integration is beyond the scope of this book, but we can look at some of the core principles and a few snippets of code.

Compared to a wire transfer journey, the major difference with direct debit is that we can perform the entire process without ever leaving the Robo-advisor. This is because we can use APIs from providers such as Plaid and Stripe to initiate a direct debit transaction. In America, direct debit happens via the **Automated Clearing House** (**ACH**) network.

ACH is a payment network that was started by American banks in the early 70s (Nacha). Since 2016, ACH has supported same-day payments. The basic process for setting up an ACH payment involves a few steps and several providers, even before we get into the technology needed. Our Robo-advisor would be the so-called originator, while two banks send and receive the actual money. In this scenario, those would be the investor's bank of choice, and the custodian bank of your Robo-advisor. Finally, there is the ACH operator, which takes care of this messaging traffic between banks. Unless you want to handle the bank account data yourself, you can potentially outsource this to a third party. Plaid supports a growing list of online brokers that can provide this service. If that happens to be your custodian, it's all the sweeter. Here's an overview of the process from Plaid:

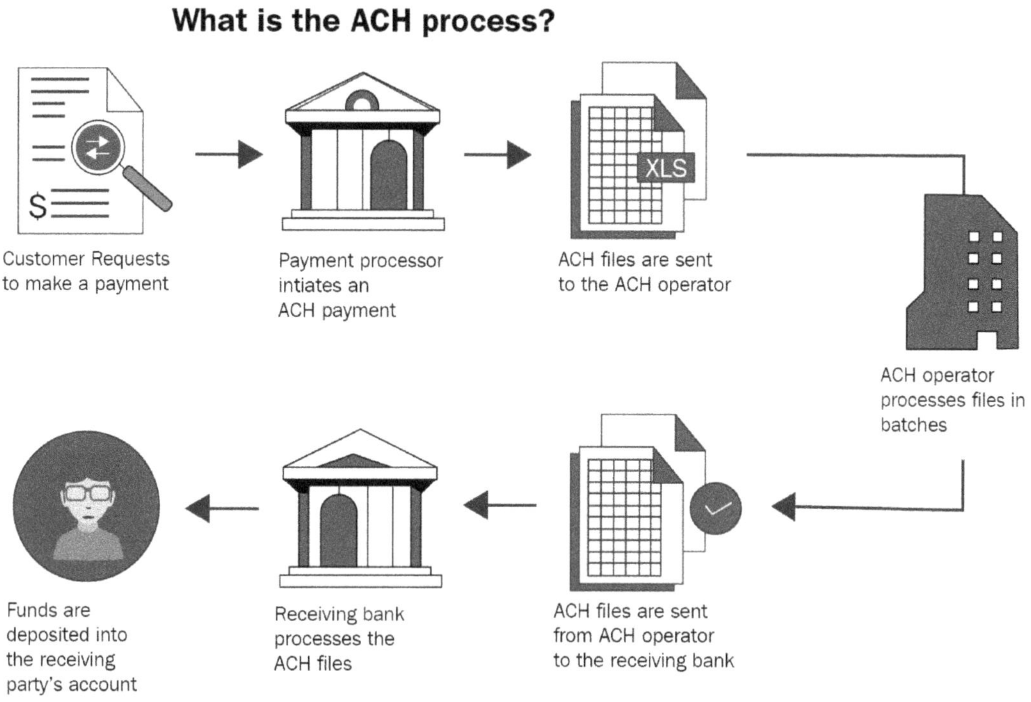

What is the ACH process?

Customer Requests to make a payment

Payment processor intiates an ACH payment

ACH files are sent to the ACH operator

ACH operator processes files in batches

Funds are deposited into the receiving party's account

Receiving bank processes the ACH files

ACH files are sent from ACH operator to the receiving bank

Figure 11.1 – Basic ACH process (Plaid)

From the preceding diagram, all we're really doing is the first part of this process: requesting a debit from the investor to the custodian. But even that has quite a lot to make it work. The beauty of using an ACH API provider such as Plaid or Stripe, while costly, is the convenience. While ACH payments are not instantaneous, they do support nearly all, if not 100% of, banks in America. Of course, for other countries, such platforms and providers may not be available, in which case you must default back to wire transfers.

Let's move forward to look at Plaid as an example of ACH integration. These steps are naturally specific to Plaid itself in America, so if you're using another provider or using Plaid in another country, this may be quite different for you. The core capability of the process is offered by Plaid Link, which is effectively an embedded UI that lets the end user securely log in and move money from their own account to the intended receiver. In our case, the investor would use Plaid Link within your Robo-advisor frontend and choose a bank, an account, and an amount to move to the custodian. This is what a standard implementation flow would look like with Plaid:

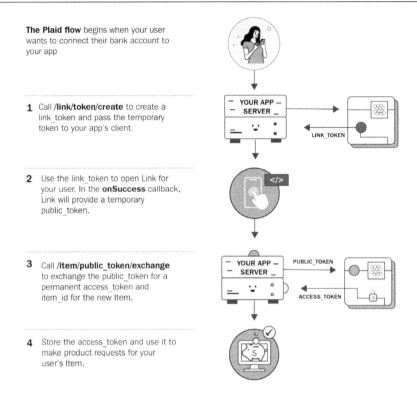

The Plaid flow begins when your user wants to connect their bank account to your app

1   Call **/link/token/create** to create a link_token and pass the temporary token to your app's client.

2   Use the link_token to open Link for your user. In the **onSuccess** callback, Link will provide a temporary public_token.

3   Call **/item/public_token/exchange** to exchange the public_token for a permanent access_token and item_id for the new Item.

4   Store the access_token and use it to make product requests for your user's Item.

Figure 11.2 – Basic Plaid workflow for ACH (the Plaid API)

A similar product solution is now being offered by Stripe, called Financial Connections. In the following screenshot, you can see how their embedded UI would display inside your app or website to link an external bank account to your Robo-advisor:

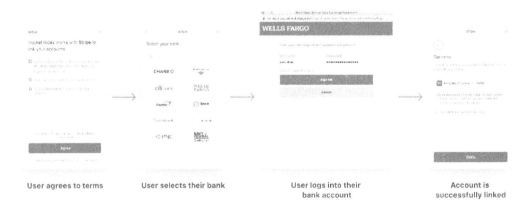

User agrees to terms   User selects their bank   User logs into their bank account   Account is successfully linked

Figure 11.3 – Example embedded UI flow for ACH (Stripe)

While Plaid does have a module for Python, they do not offer Plaid Link for Python. This is because Python is rarely (if ever) used as a frontend technology. Thus, we will only be able to demonstrate certain aspects of the process. However, it is entirely possible to communicate with the Plaid API using Python, which would take the role of the app server in *Figure 11.2*. If you are building a Robo-advisor platform for consumers, then you will need to build an app or website frontend, which is beyond the scope of this book.

You can install the Python module for Plaid using the following code:

```
!pip install plaid-python
```

Once installed, you would immediately need API credentials from Plaid, which you can request through their website. It's free and all you need is to verify an email address, and you'll have your API keys in less than a minute. Assuming you have the credentials, you can use the Python module objects to connect to the Plaid API:

```
import plaid
from plaid.api import plaid_api

configuration = plaid.Configuration(
    host=plaid.Environment.Sandbox,
    api_key={
        'clientId': "123",
        'secret': "abc",
    }
)


api_client = plaid.ApiClient(configuration)
client = plaid_api.PlaidApi(api_client)
```

In the preceding code, you simply need to replace your own credentials to start building a sandbox application. A sandbox allows you to create test transactions without the need to move real money while writing code, which would be risky and possibly illegal.

Once you've created your instance of `PlaidApi`, you can browse the available functions and find their documentation on the Plaid Developer website:

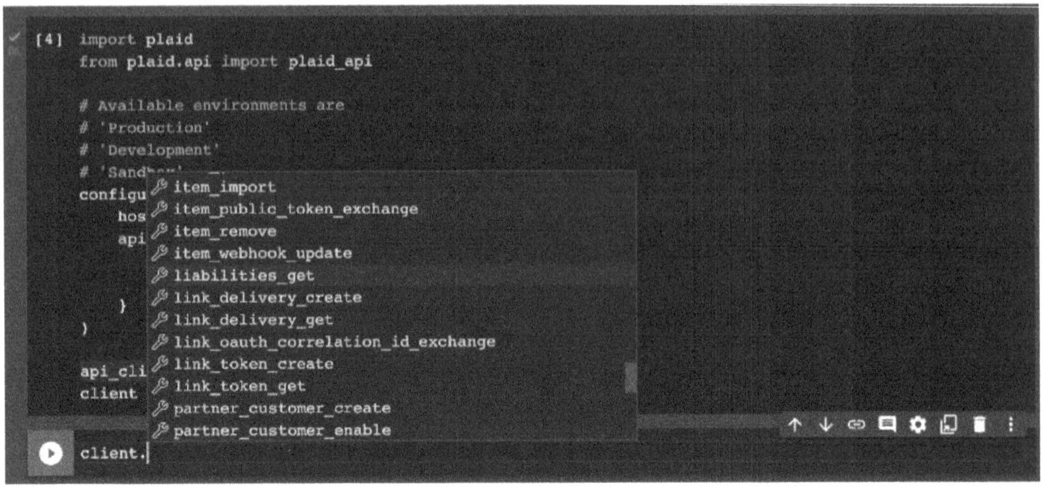

Figure 11.4 – Browsing the available Plaid API functions

One of the key concepts here is that of tokens. These are effectively encrypted credentials you will use to access various features. Because Link is how we gain access to external accounts, that is where we would naturally start. This is what the process should look like, using some example code snippets from Plaid:

1. Obtain a Link token by calling /link/token/create:

```
from plaid.model.country_code import CountryCode
from plaid.model.link_token_create_request import
LinkTokenCreateRequest
from plaid.model.link_token_create_request_user import
LinkTokenCreateRequestUser
from plaid.model.products import Products
import time

CLIENT_NAME = 'Plaid Test'

request = LinkTokenCreateRequest(
        products=[Products('auth'),
        Products('transactions')],
        client_name=CLIENT_NAME,
        country_codes=[CountryCode('GB')],
        language='en',
        user=LinkTokenCreateRequestUser(
```

```
        client_user_id=str(time.time())
      )
   )
response = client.link_token_create(request)
link_token = response['link_token']
```

2. Initialize Link in the UI by passing in `link_token`. When your user completes the Link flow, Link will pass back a public token.

   As mentioned earlier, because there is no Link UI for Python, we can only simulate *step 2* using the sandbox:

   ```
   from plaid.model.sandbox_public_token_create_request
   import SandboxPublicTokenCreateRequest
   from plaid.model.item_public_token_exchange_request
   import ItemPublicTokenExchangeRequest
   from plaid.model.products import Products

   SANDBOX_INSTITUTION = 'ins_109508'

   pt_request = SandboxPublicTokenCreateRequest(
           institution_id=SANDBOX_INSTITUTION,
           initial_products=[Products('auth')]
      )

   pt_response = client.sandbox_public_token_create(
       pt_request)

   exchange_request = ItemPublicTokenExchangeRequest(
       public_token=pt_response['public_token']
   )
   ```

3. Exchange the public token for an access token by calling `/item/public_token/exchange`:

   ```
   import plaid
   from plaid.model.item_public_token_exchange_request
   import ItemPublicTokenExchangeRequest

   exchange_request = ItemPublicTokenExchangeRequest(
       public_token=pt_response['public_token']
   ```

```
)
exchange_response = client.item_public_token_
exchange(exchange_request)
access_token = exchange_response['access_token']
```

4. The access token can then be used to call Plaid endpoints to get information about accounts and initiate transfers. First, let's get the account from Link:

```
from plaid.model.account_type import AccountType
from plaid.model.accounts_get_request import
AccountsGetRequest

accounts_request = AccountsGetRequest(
    access_token=access_token
)
accounts_response = client.accounts_get(accounts_request)

account = next(
    acct for acct in accounts_response['accounts'] if
acct['type'] == AccountType('depository'))

account_id = account['account_id']
```

5. Now, we can put all of these together to initiate an ACH direct debit transfer:

```
from plaid.model.bank_transfer_create_request import
BankTransferCreateRequest
from plaid.model.bank_transfer_network import
BankTransferNetwork
from plaid.model.bank_transfer_idempotency_key import
BankTransferIdempotencyKey
from plaid.model.bank_transfer_type import
BankTransferType
from plaid.model.bank_transfer_user import
BankTransferUser
from plaid.model.ach_class import ACHClass
from random import random

bt_request = BankTransferCreateRequest(
        idempotency_
```

```
        key=BankTransferIdempotencyKey(str(random())),
            access_token=access_token,
            account_id=account_id,
            type=BankTransferType('credit'),
            network=BankTransferNetwork('ach'),
            amount='1.00',
            iso_currency_code='USD',
            description='test',
            user=BankTransferUser(legal_name='Firstname
Lastname'),
            ach_class=ACHClass('ppd'),
            custom_tag='',
        )


    bt_response = client.bank_transfer_create(bt_request)
```

If you get an error such as the following, it's because you're on the free tier of the API and need to upgrade to a paid plan to access certain products within Plaid:

```
ApiException: (400)
Reason: Bad Request
HTTP response headers: HTTPHeaderDict({'Server': 'nginx',
'Date': 'Sun, 20 Nov 2022 10:29:34 GMT', 'Content-Type':
'application/json; charset=utf-8', 'Content-Length': '342',
'Connection': 'keep-alive', 'plaid-version': '2020-09-14'})
HTTP response body: {
  "display_message": null,
  "documentation_url": "https://plaid.com/
docs/?ref=error#invalid-input-errors",
  "error_code": "INVALID_PRODUCT",
  "error_message": "client is not authorized to access the
following products: [\"bank_transfer\"]",
  "error_type": "INVALID_INPUT",
  "request_id": "fSbWQAB5AZ1ULrN",
  "suggested_action": null
}
```

Logically, if you need to build this integration for your Robo-advisor, now is the time to upgrade your Plaid API plan. To wrap this up, let's look at how we'll confirm when the ACH payment has been made.

Validating direct debit transfers

There is really no difference here compared to wire transfers. Once the ACH process has been initiated, you will still need to confirm the funds received via the custodian, not Plaid. It's likely that you will need to scrape the same SOD file just like with wire transfers.

That wraps up our exploration of account funding mechanisms, and how we can use third-party providers to implement direct debit transfers.

Summary

In this chapter, we added one last missing piece to enable transactions: putting money into our accounts. We started off by looking at the simplest approach, which is wire transfers, and how to validate them with the custodian. We spent most of the chapter on introducing direct debit ACH payments, and how we can use Plaid's API to build such capabilities for our Robo-advisor.

We tried snippets of code from Plaid's Python module and sandbox API to build a core token workflow that enables an investor to log into their own bank account and choose an amount to transfer to your Robo-advisor.

By now, you should have sufficient knowledge to explore the potential account funding mechanisms and providers available for your country and use case. For direct debit transfers, you now have a basic understanding of the process and effort involved.

Now that we have an account set up with funds inside, in the next chapter, we will attempt to make our first investment transaction.

Further reading

You might be interested in reading some extra information related to the topics discussed in this chapter. Here are a few links to some of the external resources:

- Nacha. *History of Nacha and the ACH Network*. Accessed online 20.11.2022. `https://www.nacha.org/content/history-nacha-and-ach-network`

- Plaid. *What is ACH? The ultimate guide to ACH payments*. Accessed online 20.11.2022. `https://plaid.com/resources/ach/what-is-ach/`

- The Plaid API. *Link overview*. Accessed online 20.11.2022. `https://plaid.com/docs/link/`

- Stripe. *Financial Connections fundamentals*. Accessed online 20.11.2022. `https://stripe.com/docs/financial-connections/fundamentals`

12
Order Management and Execution

There's no question, this is going to be the most complicated part of your Robo-advisor. I'll do my best to inform you of key concepts, logic, and concerns, but much will be left to you to work out for yourself in collaboration with your broker.

We will kick off the chapter by introducing some key terms and concepts required for implementing basic order management processes. To get hands-on with orders, we will finally connect our goals, portfolios, and accounts. We will then set up the basic classes and class methods for orders, split orders, and master orders.

Once we have the basic objects in hand, we will implement a full seven-step order management workflow. This will cover splitting orders to the product level, aggregating those into master orders, and finally allocating filled orders back to accounts and Goals.

I should caveat that this chapter, in particular, is where 1,000 small things can go wrong, resulting in erroneous trades or mismatches in reconciliation. The code presented in the chapters should be thought of as pseudocode, or instructional code, meant to highlight certain concepts or methods. For the sake of brevity and focus, we do not cover validation and testing which are a crucial part of any transactional implementation. We have purposely omitted the rounding of units and amounts in this chapter, which is left for you to implement based on the specifications of your broker and custodian. This is crucial in order to avoid small fractional mismatches between the Robo-advisor and custodian.

In a production-scale consumer platform, it really starts to matter how efficient and error-resistant your code is. This is especially true of the broker interface, which should be subject to extensive testing, all of which is outside the scope of this book. For reference, an average broker integration might take up to 6 months of development, of which at least 2 months are just for testing.

Thankfully, brokers will not trust your software to be correct. So, they'll provide tests to prove your software implements their trading rules and correctly handles the multitude of exceptions that can and will happen in trading systems. If we were to cover all that in this book, this chapter alone would be a whole book's worth of code. Hence, consider this a starting point on a long journey.

In this chapter, we're going to cover the following topics:

- What is required to create an order

- The differences between fractional and whole-share orders

- How to create an order

- Advanced order management

Technical requirements

It's important to note that one important piece of technology we have ignored is a database. In reality, whether using the Robo-advisor for yourself or building a consumer platform, you'll need to persist all these objects that you are creating and interacting with. For a personal project, the simplest approach would be to persist your data in a JSON or Pickle file, but a more robust solution would be the sqlite3 database that comes packaged with Python itself. Third-party modules such as pydapper make it easier to store and query our existing custom classes by using them as Python dataclass models directly. You could get fancier with a NoSQL solution such as MongoDB, which uses dictionaries that can be easily passed to APIs as JSON files.

The other note to make here is on APIs themselves. As we are not implementing a frontend, we are interacting directly through Python code in all our examples. If that isn't ideal for your Robo-advisor, then you will want to deploy the Python capabilities as an API that your frontend code can easily consume. Creating APIs doesn't need to be very difficult, at least on a small scale. By using the FastAPI Python module, after installing with pip as usual, you can do it in just a few lines of code:

```
from fastapi import FastAPI
app = FastAPI()
@app.get("/my-first-api")
def hello():
    return {"Hello world!"}
```

This, however, will not run inside Colab. APIs need to be deployed on a dedicated server, which, for the purposes of testing, can be your own laptop, but not Colab, which runs somewhere on Google's cloud. This is beyond the scope of our book, but check out the *Further reading* section for a decent guide (Fernandez). For production-scale consumer platforms, you might want to look at Flask or Django instead and deploy those on Heroku, Azure, or AWS.

Now, let's get back to work on these orders.

Requirements for creating an order

Let's start with some basic information required for orders, and work our way up from there. Fundamentally, an order is pretty simple. You just want to buy or sell some type of investment product. Let's break it down.

This isn't an exhaustive list, as it will depend on your broker and local regulations, which are always subject to change, yet you would likely require, at least, the following:

- **Transaction type**: We would require at least **buy** and **sell** order types, but in certain scenarios, a **switch** would be helpful, which just means we change from one equivalent product to another as opposed to cashing out.

- **Order type**: The two main order types supported by brokers are called **limit orders** and **market orders**. Robo-advisors always use market orders, so we don't need to track this per order.

- **Product**: What are you buying? In our case, it's not just one product ticker, but a whole portfolio at a time. This means that one order for our Robo-advisor becomes a series of orders for the broker. We will, therefore, need information on the portfolio attached to the order. This includes the **exchange-traded fund** (**ETF**) tickers, allocations or weights per ticker, price per ticker, and any limitations imposed by the broker or fund provider on minimum amounts and transaction fees.

- **Amount**: How much of a given investment product are you buying or selling? This could be expressed in a monetary amount or as units of the product. We'll elaborate on the differences later in this chapter. Either way, the broker will typically have some minimum order amount, which could start from $1 for ETFs.

- **Status**: We need some way to track what's happening with the order, from being generated on the Robo-advisor to tracking its processing by the broker.

- **Account**: Which account is making this transaction? For simplicity's sake, we would assume the same account holds the cash balance needed to settle the transaction.

- **Goal**: Because we are building on the basis of Goal-based investing, every order would trace back to a Goal. We'll explore this relationship in more detail later on.

It's worth noting that most brokers would support much more complicated order information because they are required for advanced products such as margin, futures, and options. For the purposes of Robo-advisory, we don't need those.

Differences between fractional and whole-share orders

When it comes to trading financial products, the traditional method would be to trade whole shares. This means that the broker would expect orders with integers, not fractions of units. For example, if one ETF costs $100, then that would impose that any portfolio including that ETF could only make orders of at least $100. Now, if you have 10 similar ETFs in your portfolio, your minimum account and investment are effectively $1,000. This is a barrier for a lot of people to start investing.

Luckily, innovation has taken place, and many online brokers now support notional or fractional trading. Now, you can place orders in exact dollar amounts. So now, you can buy a slice of that $1,000 portfolio with just $1. The way it works is that your $1 gets split down into fractional units. Instead of owning one unit of each ETF, you only get 0.01 units. This method is what we will be using in this chapter.

Creating an order

Before we can create an order, we need to catch up on previous chapters and set up some prerequisites. First, let's create a basic Account class that we may have populated with information from our custodian API in *Chapters 10* and *11*:

```
class AccountType():
  def __init__(self, value: str):
    if not value in("Taxable", "Roth IRA", "Traditional IRA"):
      raise ValueError("Allowed types: Taxable, Roth IRA,
Traditional IRA")
    self.value = value
  def __eq__(self, other):
    return self.value == other.value


class AccountStatus():
  def __init__(self, value: str):
    if not value in("PENDING", "IN_REVIEW", "APPROVED",
"REJECTED", "SUSPENDED"):
      raise ValueError("Allowed statuses: PENDING, IN_REVIEW,
APPROVED, REJECTED, SUSPENDED")
    self.value = value
  def __eq__(self, other):
    return self.value == other.value


class Account():
  def __init__(self, number: str, accountType: AccountType,
accountStatus: AccountStatus, cashBalance: float=0.0):
    self.goals = []
    self.number = number
    self.cashBalance = cashBalance
```

```
    self.accountType = accountType
    self.accountStatus = accountStatus
```

For the sake of this exercise, we just need a few pieces of information about accounts, instead of complete onboarding and KYC information. However, we have modeled additional classes to keep track of the account type and account status when making our orders. To make it practical, we have added an override method for comparing these objects. In Python, you can do this by defining your own __eq__ () function. Finally, we've also added a mapping to Goals here. By adding an empty list, we allow connecting multiple Goals to our account going forward. Here is an example diagram of how Goals and accounts map to various account types:

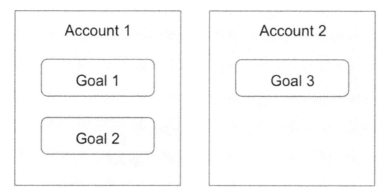

Figure 12.1 – Relationship between Goals, investment accounts, and external accounts

For this chapter, we will assume the necessary funds from the external bank account are already in place, as established in *Chapter 11, Funding Your Account*. Next, we will tie back a portfolio to our Goal object from *Chapter 6, Goal-Based Investing*:

```
class Goal:
    def __init__(self, name, targetYear, targetValue, portfolio:
Portfolio=None, initialContribution=0, monthlyContribution=0,
priority=""):
        self.name = name
        self.targetYear = targetYear
        self.targetValue = targetValue
        self.initialContribution = initialContribution
        self.monthlyContribution = monthlyContribution
        if not (priority == "") and not (priority in ["Dreams",
"Wishes", "Wants", "Needs"]):
            raise ValueError("Wrong value set for Priority.")
        self.priority = priority
```

```
    self.portfolio = portfolio

  def getGoalProbabilities(self):
    if (self.priority == ""):
            raise ValueError("No value set for Priority.")
    import pandas as pd
    lookupTable=pd.read_csv("/content/Data/Goal Probability
Table.csv")
    match = (lookupTable["Realize"] == self.priority)
    minProb = lookupTable["MinP"][(match)]
    maxProb = lookupTable["MaxP"][(match)]
    return minProb.values[0], maxProb.values[0]
```

This ensures that each Goal will have either zero or one portfolio tied to it. What we're going for is a relationship that looks like the following diagram:

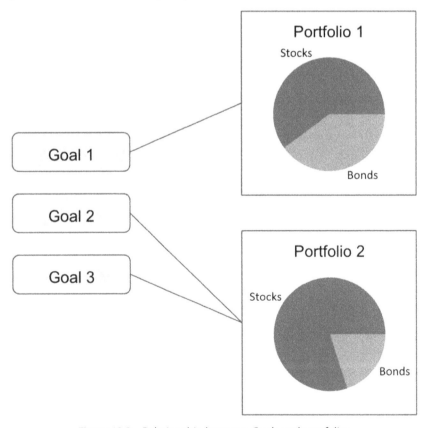

Figure 12.2 – Relationship between Goals and portfolios

As our Robo-advisor will have a limited number of model portfolios, but an unlimited number of Goals, some Goals will end up using the same model portfolio.

While we're at it, let's add an additional field to our `Allocation` class so we can keep track of any holdings we may have:

```python
class Allocation:
    def __init__(self, ticker, percentage):
        self.ticker = ticker
        self.percentage = percentage
        self.units = 0.0
```

This won't interfere with our previous code but gives us a place to store holdings on a Goal level, as each allocation maps to a portfolio that maps to a Goal that maps to an account. Refer to the preceding diagram if you're confused.

Next, we will need a few helper objects to support our `Order` class. We can model allowed order types and statuses as separate classes with `ValueError` thrown if the correct choice is not made:

```python
class TransactionType():
    def __init__(self, value: str):
        if not value in("BUY", "SELL"):
            raise ValueError("Allowed types: BUY, SELL.")
        self.value = value
    def __eq__(self, other):
        return self.value == other.value


class OrderStatus():
    def __init__(self, value: str):
        if not value in("NEW", "PENDING", "FILLED", "REJECTED"):
            raise ValueError("Allowed statuses: NEW, PENDING, FILLED, REJECTED.")
        self.value = value
    def __eq__(self, other):
        return self.value == other.value
```

Depending on your broker, you will likely require more granular values, but these are a good starting point. Now, let's add the `Order` class:

```python
class Order:
    def __init__(self, account: Account, goal:
```

```
Goal, transactionType: TransactionType, status:
OrderStatus=OrderStatus("NEW"), dollarAmount: float=0.0):


    self.account = account
    self.transactionType = transactionType
    self.dollarAmount = dollarAmount
    self.goal = goal
    self.status = status
```

Here, we assume that the default status for any new order will be NEW, and expect new orders to be associated with an existing account and Goal. Before we can really make much use of this new class, we should add some checks to make sure the order is valid to send to a broker. We'll add these new functions into the Order class as class methods:

```
def checkAccountStatus(self) -> bool:
    if self.account.status == AccountStatus("APPROVED"):
        return True
    else:
        return False
```

The first one is simple. We just want to make sure the underlying account is ready to transact. Next, we check whether the order size is appropriate:

```
def checkOrderSize(self) -> bool:
    if self.dollarAmount > 1.00:
        return True
    else:
        return False
```

Of course, this is a simplification. In reality, you may have several different types of limitations between your platform and the broker and what makes sense in terms of fees charged for transactions between the parties. We should also check we have enough cash to make the transaction:

```
def checkBalances(self) -> bool:
    if self.transactionType == TransactionType("BUY") and self.
account.cashBalance >= self.dollarAmount:
        return True
    elif self.transactionType == TransactionType("SELL"):
        goalValue = 0.0
        for allocation in goal.portfolio.allocations:
```

```
        price = float(yf.Ticker(
            allocation.ticker).basic_info["previousClose"])
        goalValue += allocation.units * price
    if self.dollarAmount <= goalValue:
      return True
    else:
      return False
  else:
    return False
```

If we are selling, we don't need cash in the account unless there are transaction fees to be settled in cash first. What we would need to do is check whether the market value of your portfolio actually covers what you're trying to sell. Again, the real-world complexities will vary.

The last check we'll need is whether or not the markets are actually open to trade. There is a sidebar here to discuss how orders will be processed by the broker. Besides technical limitations on how orders can be passed via API or file transfer, there are likely fee benefits to making orders in batches instead of piecemeal. This choice is left for you to make.

To know whether markets are open, we'll need an up-to-date market calendar. There are many sources, one of which may be your broker themselves. For the sake of the exercise, we'll use yet another Python module. You can install it with the following:

```
!pip install pandas_market_calendars
```

Once installed, you can create a simple helper function to confirm market availability, either as a separate function or by adding it to the Order class:

```
def isMarketOpen():
  from datetime import datetime, timedelta
  import pandas_market_calendars as mcal

  previousday = datetime.now() - timedelta(5)
  nextday = datetime.now() + timedelta(5)
  nyse = mcal.get_calendar('NYSE')
  sched = nyse.schedule(start_date=previousday,
    end_date=nextday)

  return nyse.is_open_now(sched)
```

On most weekdays, the NYSE market is open from 8:00 A.M. to 05:00 P.M. local time in New York. So, depending on when you're reading this, the market may or may not be open, but try it either way.

Now, we can put all our helper functions together into one convenient class method:

```
def checkOrderViability(self) -> bool:
    if self.checkAccountStatus() and self.checkOrderSize() and
        self.checkBalances() and isMarketOpen():
      return True
    else:
      return False
```

This means orders are only viable to send to the broker if all the conditions are met. This also makes it easier to maintain these methods independently, as the amount and specificity of those conditions can grow quite large.

We can now try this all out by setting up some test objects:

```
myPortfolio = Portfolio("VTI TLT IEI GLD DBC", expectedReturn =
0.05, portfolioName = "Moderate", riskBucket = 3)
myGoal = Goal(name="Vacation", targetYear=2027,
targetValue=10000, priority="Dreams", portfolio=myPortfolio)
myAccount=Account(number="123456789", accountType="Taxable",
accountStatus=AccountStatus("APPROVED"), cashBalance=10.0)
myAccount.goals.append(myGoal)


newOrder = Order(account=myAccount, goal=myGoal,
transactionType=TransactionType("BUY"), dollarAmount=10.0)
newOrder.checkOrderViability()
```

Depending on your local time, this may return True or False. This gives all the basic pieces we'll need to look at in an end-to-end order management workflow.

Advanced order management

The complexity of order management depends on a few factors. One is the chosen or available account structure, where a master trading account is preferable. This allows us to aggregate trades from multiple orders for cost efficiency. Goals add quite a lot of complexity as they are effectively virtual sub-accounts under individual accounts. This means, we have to track orders under a Goal, not just an account, and different Goals can have different portfolios. Furthermore, since the broker and custodian are oblivious to the existence of our Goals, we must allocate filled orders ourselves back to our Goals.

If we put these factors together into a workflow, our order management workflow would look like this:

1. The investor creates an order.

2. The Robo-advisor checks the order information and rejects it if not viable.

3. The Robo-advisor splits orders from Goal to fund level.

4. The Robo-advisor aggregates orders from individual accounts to the master account.

5. The broker fills orders for the master account.

6. The Robo-advisor splits resulting allocations from master to account level.

7. The Robo-advisor splits resulting allocations from account to Goal level.

We'll now look at some simple implementations of these individual steps. We've already covered *step 1* and *step 2*. Let's assume the market is open, and the order is viable.

Now, let's split some orders.

Splitting orders

If we pick up the process from our first example order, the first task at hand is to figure out what actual ETFs we are buying here. That means converting the order amount in dollars to dollar amounts for the underlying ETFs tucked away inside our portfolio that is tied to our Goal. That sounds complicated, so let's break it down.

First, let's find our portfolio again. If we've lost track of everything else, we can recover that directly from our `Order` object. Thanks to all the work we've done previously, we can do that with one simple line of code:

```
newOrder.goal.portfolio.printPortfolio()
```

You should see a nice printout of the portfolio we created as follows:

```
Portfolio Name: Moderate
Risk Bucket: 3
Expected Return: 0.05
Expected Risk: 0.09834845279995
Allocations:
Ticker: TLT, Percentage: 0.08112
Ticker: IEI, Percentage: 0.2053
Ticker: DBC, Percentage: 0.0
Ticker: GLD, Percentage: 0.37005
Ticker: VTI, Percentage: 0.34353
```

So, what we're after is the list of allocations, so that we can figure out the amount of TLT, GLD, and the other ETFs to buy from the broker. We can access that list again using our previous work. This time, we want to calculate a dollar amount per ETF:

```
for allocation in newOrder.goal.portfolio.allocations:
  print(newOrder.transactionType.value + ": " +
    allocation.ticker + ", $" + str(
        allocation.percentage * newOrder.dollarAmount))
```

You should see something like this:

```
BUY: IEI, $2.053
BUY: TLT, $0.8111999999999999
BUY: GLD, $3.7005
BUY: DBC, $0.0
BUY: VTI, $3.4353
```

To make this practical, we could create a new helper class for this kind of split order, and even add a class method underneath the Order class to create them for us:

```
class SplitOrder:
  def __init__(self, originalOrder: Order, ticker: str,
dollarAmount: float):
    self.originalOrder = originalOrder
    self.ticker = ticker
    self.dollarAmount = dollarAmount
```

Now, let's create another helper function that you can place under the Order class:

```
def split(self) -> list:
    splits = []
    for allocation in self.goal.portfolio.allocations:
      if (allocation.percentage > 0):
        splits.append(SplitOrder(originalOrder=self,
            ticker=allocation.ticker, dollarAmount=
                allocation.percentage * self.dollarAmount))
    return splits
```

Now, we have the ability to produce a list of split orders at the ETF level from a new order created for a given Goal. Pretty decent. We just want to filter out any zero allocations to avoid trying to place orders for zero dollars at the broker. Remember that in order to use new functions added after an object was instantiated, we need to re-create the object. So, let's try this:

```
newOrder = Order(account=myAccount, goal=myGoal,
transactionType=TransactionType("BUY"), dollarAmount=10.0)
splitOrders = newOrder.split()
```

We can confirm that we got something useful and that we can always recoup the original order and even which Goal it belongs to:

```
print(splitOrders[0].ticker)
print(splitOrders[0].originalOrder.goal.name)
```

You should see a similar output:

```
IEI
Vacation
```

Now, we have a bunch of split orders for one Goal. The next step is to group together multiple split orders from multiple Goals to aggregate them into a master order.

Order aggregation

If we assume, as we should, that trades are executed on a master account, then the broker will expect a list of orders at that level. The broker doesn't know or care about our Goals, portfolios, or even our investor accounts. So, let's set up the basic class and helper functions as usual:

```
import pandas as pd
class MasterOrder:
  def __init__(self, status: OrderStatus=OrderStatus("NEW")):

    self.splitOrders = []
    self.masterTable = pd.DataFrame(columns=[
        'Account','Symbol','Type','DollarAmount'])
    self.status = status

  def addSplitOrder(self, splitOrder: SplitOrder):
    self.splitOrders.append(splitOrder)

  def aggregate(self) -> pd.DataFrame:
    for split in self.splitOrders:
```

```
        new_row = {'Account':split.originalOrder.account.
number,'Symbol':split.ticker,'Type':split.originalOrder.
transactionType.value,'DollarAmount':split.dollarAmount}
        self.masterTable = self.masterTable.append(new_row,
ignore_index=True)


    return self.masterTable.groupby([
        'Symbol','Type']).sum().reset_index()
```

The first thing to note is that we're going to keep our own record of these orders in a DataFrame object, which is like a spreadsheet or database table that we can work with directly. We predefine the columns, even though the table itself is empty initially. The two class methods allow us to first add orders that we split previously, and then, in turn, aggregate them into one master order. The master order table rows are populated with information from the split orders, but the return value is actually a smaller table where we group the rows by symbol (ticker) and order type (buy or sell), adding together the total dollar amounts.

We can now add our split orders to the master order table by using the following code:

```
newMasterOrder = MasterOrder()
for split in splitOrders:
  newMasterOrder.addSplitOrder(split)
```

We also want to create another order to make things a bit more interesting. We'll also use a different account and Goal and then split this order too:

```
myPortfolio2 = Portfolio("VTI TLT IEI GLD DBC", expectedReturn
= 0.03, portfolioName = "Conservative", riskBucket = 2)
myGoal2 = Goal(name="Car", targetYear=2025, targetValue=5000,
priority="Dreams", portfolio=myPortfolio)
myAccount2=Account(number="987654321", accountType="Taxable",
accountStatus=AccountStatus("APPROVED"), cashBalance=20.0)
myAccount2.goals.append(myGoal2)
newOrder2 = Order(account=myAccount2, goal=myGoal2,
transactionType=TransactionType("BUY"), dollarAmount=20.0)
print(newOrder2.checkOrderViability())
splitOrders2 = newOrder2.split()
```

Now, let's add this second group of split orders to the master order, and aggregate them:

```
for split in splitOrders2:
  newMasterOrder.addSplitOrder(split)
```

```
newMasterTable = newMasterOrder.aggregate()
print(newMasterTable)
```

What you should see is this:

```
  Symbol Type  DollarAmount
0    GLD  BUY       11.1015
1    IEI  BUY        6.1590
2    TLT  BUY        2.4336
3    VTI  BUY       10.3059
```

As you can see here, we have lost a lot of information due to aggregation by product instead of single accounts or Goals, for the benefit of executing the trades at the correct master level with the broker. Now, we can save these to a file, which might be passed to the broker. In our case, this is a CSV file, but some brokers may provide an API that takes in JSON formatted orders:

```
newMasterTable.to_csv('/content/Data/MasterOrder.csv')
```

Simple as that. You can browse the file in the folder to see what it looks like. It should match the previous output:

MasterOrder.csv

	A	B	C	D
1		Symbol	Type	DollarAmount
2	0	GLD	BUY	11.1015
3	1	IEI	BUY	6.159
4	2	TLT	BUY	2.4336
5	3	VTI	BUY	10.3059

Figure 12.3 – Our output master order CSV file

Now, we've done what we needed to do and can wait for the master orders to be filled. Let's make sure we update our order statuses accordingly:

```
newMasterOrder.orderSent()
print(newMasterOrder.splitOrders[0].originalOrder.status.value)
```

You should see **PENDING** as the output. Depending on how you batch your orders, and whether the markets are open, this may happen quickly or much later. Your broker would supply you with an API to check the order status. There is a multitude of conditions on the broker side that may cause your order to be fully or partially rejected, or fully or partially filled. We will look at an example of a simple buy across two accounts, and leave the rest to you to implement and test.

Now, let's imagine the broker returns our filled orders in a CSV file in the following format:

	A	B	C	D	E
1	OrderID	Symbol	Type	Units	Price
2	0 GLD	BUY		0.068015562	163.22
3	1 IEI	BUY		0.053417173	115.3
4	2 TLT	BUY		0.023650146	102.9
5	3 VTI	BUY		0.051135755	201.54

Figure 12.4 – Example filled orders from the broker

What we should assume here is that the broker is able to maintain the index of the order file we sent, which is important for the next part.

Lastly, let's just add another class method that updates that all our orders are filled. Remember that you will need to add further logic for partially filled orders:

```
def orderFilled(self):
    newStatus = OrderStatus("FILLED")
    self.status = newStatus
    for split in self.splitOrders:
        split.originalOrder.status = newStatus
```

Now, we can go ahead and update our order statuses:

```
newMasterOrder.orderFilled()
```

The next job is allocation, which we're ready to tackle now.

Order allocation

Now, we need to reverse what we did earlier and decrypt the filled master account orders into our investor accounts and their associated Goals. Let's read that CSV into our Python code for processing:

```
filledMasterOrder = pd.read_csv(
    '/content/ Data/MasterOrder_Filled.csv')
filledMasterOrder = filledMasterOrder.set_index(
    filledMasterOrder.columns[0])
print(filledMasterOrder)
```

We want to make sure we're maintaining the same index as when we sent the orders out, by using the OrderID column. The output should look like this:

```
         Symbol  Type     Units     Price
OrderID
0           GLD   BUY  0.068016   163.22
1           IEI   BUY  0.053417   115.30
2           TLT   BUY  0.023650   102.90
3           VTI   BUY  0.051136   201.54
```

Before we go further, let's remind ourselves of the split orders we started with. We can still access those, as we stored them inside the master order:

```
Print(newMasterOrder.masterTable)
```

You should see the following output:

```
     Account  Symbol  Type  DollarAmount
0   123456789    TLT   BUY        0.8112
1   123456789    VTI   BUY        3.4353
2   123456789    GLD   BUY        3.7005
3   123456789    IEI   BUY        2.0530
4   987654321    TLT   BUY        1.6224
5   987654321    VTI   BUY        6.8706
6   987654321    GLD   BUY        7.4010
7   987654321    IEI   BUY        4.1060
```

This will be useful for comparing our results after allocation is done. Now, we need another class method under `MasterOrder` to do just that:

```
def allocateAccounts(self, filledMasterOrderFile: pd.DataFrame)
-> pd.DataFrame:
    accountTable =
pd.DataFrame(columns=['Account','Symbol','Type','Units'],
index=self.masterTable.index)
    for index, row in filledMasterOrderFile.iterrows():
        ordersToAllocate = self.masterTable[(
            self.masterTable['Symbol'] == row['Symbol']) & (
            self.masterTable['Type'] == row['Type'])]
        totalValue = float(ordersToAllocate.
groupby(['Symbol','Type'])['DollarAmount'].sum()[0])
        for index2, row2 in ordersToAllocate.iterrows():
            unitsAllocated = (row2['
                DollarAmount'] / totalValue) * row['Units']
            new_row =
{'Account':row2['Account'],'Symbol':row2['Symbol'],
'Type':row2['Type'],'Units':unitsAllocated}
            accountTable.iloc[index2] = new_row
            self.splitOrders[index2].units = unitsAllocated
    return accountTable
```

We first created another DataFrame, which we will be passing to the custodian, and once again, they have no knowledge of our Goals, just the accounts for each investor and which positions they hold. Next, we need to compare the filled order to our master order table. We sum together all dollar amounts to calculate the correct ratio of units to allocate. While we're at it, we also update our split-order objects, which will make it easier to track back to our Goals for the next step.

It's very important to note that this allocation may not always come out to exactly zero. The reason is that brokers may operate at a limited precision for fractional trading. This may result in extra cents or dollars left over. Luckily, the broker will mandate a specific rule, such as priority by the highest last digit. That fun is left for you to figure out.

Now, let's see this in action:

```
accountAllocations = newMasterOrder.
allocateAccounts(filledMasterOrder)
print(accountAllocations)
```

You should see a similar output, which you can compare to the earlier master table printout:

```
     Account  Symbol  Type     Units
0  123456789     TLT   BUY   0.007883
1  123456789     VTI   BUY   0.017045
2  123456789     GLD   BUY   0.022672
3  123456789     IEI   BUY   0.017806
4  987654321     TLT   BUY   0.015767
5  987654321     VTI   BUY   0.034091
6  987654321     GLD   BUY   0.045344
7  987654321     IEI   BUY   0.035611
```

We have now successfully converted dollars into units via the broker, hooray! We can now pass these account allocations to the custodian, so they can update their records for any and all holdings at the individual account level:

```
accountAllocations.to_csv('/content/ Data/Account_Allocations.
csv')
```

Once you receive the next SOD file from the custodian, you need to reconcile that your values match across accounts. We'll leave that for you since we're in a generous mood.

All that's left for us to do now is to update positions for our Goals. Let's wrap this up by adding a final class method for allocating to our Goals:

```
def allocateGoals(self):
    for order in self.splitOrders:
        portfolioAllocations = order.originalOrder.goal.
portfolio.allocations
        for idx, item in enumerate(portfolioAllocations):
            if item.ticker == order.ticker and order.originalOrder.
transactionType == TransactionType("BUY"):
                order.originalOrder.goal.portfolio.allocations[idx].
units += order.units
            elif item.ticker == order.ticker and order.
originalOrder.transactionType == TransactionType("SELL"):
                order.originalOrder.goal.portfolio.allocations[idx].
units -= order.units
```

Conceptually, this is similar to what we did with accounts but, thankfully, we already updated units for our split orders so we can pick up from there. We first find the matching ticker for each allocation, and then use the transaction type (buy or sell) to add or subtract units from the existing holdings.

We can run this code and see what happens:

```
newMasterOrder.allocateGoals()
print(str(myGoal.portfolio.allocations[0].ticker) + ": " +
str(myGoal.portfolio.allocations[0].units))
```

The output should match the allocation table:

```
TLT: 0.007883382
```

Well, there we have it. We had to skip a ton of intricate details that you may need to wrestle with your broker, starting from various fee structures to complying with their trading procedures since it's beyond the scope of this book. I hope this at least gives you a handle on the concepts and core logic needed to tackle that considerable challenge ahead.

This concludes our hands-on exercises to manage orders.

Summary

In this chapter, we really went for the proverbial jugular of our Robo-advisor. While many consider that rebalancing or financial planning is what defines a Robo-advisor, most of your effort and headaches will focus on order management. There's no way around it; it's a beast.

We started by introducing some key terms and concepts required for implementing basic order management processes. We established that fractional trading is the way to go, as it enables us to trade with effectively no minimum limits on orders.

To get hands-on with orders, we started with some updates to previous classes to make sure we can connect our Goals, portfolios, and accounts. We then set up the basic Order class and added some helper class methods for checking whether orders were valid. To do that, we added a handy Python module for checking market opening hours.

Once we had a basic order in play, we went right into splitting orders as part of a seven-step order management workflow. First, we split Goal-level orders into the portfolio level to find how much of each ETF to buy. We then aggregated those orders into the master account level for processing by the broker.

Having received our filled orders back from the broker, we then allocated those orders back to accounts for our custodian to update their records, and Goal level, for us to update our own.

This chapter concludes *Part 2* of the book, where we have built all the major blocks of capabilities needed to stand up a Robo-advisor. The next and final part will focus on the capabilities required to operate a live Robo-advisor, starting with performance reporting.

Further reading

You might be interested in reading some extra information related to the topics discussed in this chapter:

* Fernandez, Ander. *How to create an API in Python.* Accessed online 26.11.2022. `https://anderfernandez.com/en/blog/how-to-create-api-python/`

Part 3: Running and Operating Your Own Robo-Advisor

Robo-advisors are not manual algorithms but are automated to ensure the portfolio is consistently in good standing. This section covers the additional requirements to run and operate a Robo-advisor continuously.

This section has the following chapters:

- *Chapter 13, Performance Reporting*
- *Chapter 14, Rebalancing*
- *Chapter 15, Dividends and Fee Management*
- *Chapter 16, Regulations for Robo-Advisors*

Performance Reporting

In this chapter, we will build on what we previously completed with portfolios in *Chapter 8, Model Portfolio Construction*. Once you've created a portfolio and invested real money, your main concern will be to track your investment. This is generally referred to as *performance reporting*. We will look at some key concepts required to make basic calculations for **Profit and Loss (P&L)**. From there, we will start building some code to calculate and visualize performance in different ways. As always, we will put together all our code in a set of reusable functions that can be added to your Robo-advisor.

By the end of the chapter, you'll have built basic implementations of the necessary algorithms to track your portfolio performance in Python.

In this chapter, we're going to cover the following topics:

- Learning how to calculate P&L for your portfolio
- Learning how to compare portfolio performance to a benchmark

Calculating P&L for your portfolio

Before we start writing more code, let's cover a few basic terms and formulas that will come in handy in this chapter:

- **Time-Weighted Rate of Return (TWRR)**: This is the simplest method of projecting potential portfolio returns. This approach ignores any additional cash coming in or out of your portfolio. The formula for TWRR is as follows:

$$R = \frac{EV - (BV + C)}{BV + C}$$

Here:

- R is the return for the period
- EV is the end value for the period
- BV is the beginning value for the period
- C is the added cash flow for the period

If we combine multiple periods, we can calculate TWRR as follows:

$$TWRR_n = (1 + R_1) \times ... \times (1 + R_n) - 1$$

Here:

- $TWRR_n$ is the TWRR at period n

- R_1 is the return for period 1

- R_n is the return for period n

- **Money-Weighted Rate of Return** (**MWRR**): This is a more sophisticated version of TWRR, whereby we factor in cash flows coming in and going out of your investment. With MWRR, the timing of cash flows will impact P&L; hence, it may skew the perception of your platform due to how users fund their accounts and Goals. This method is more relevant for other scenarios such as hedge funds that control the timing of cash flows of a large fund with many investors. If you wish to use MWRR instead for your Robo-advisor, the implementation is left to you.

Due to the preceding reasoning, we will focus on TWRR for our implementation. To calculate P&L using TWRR, we will need a history of cash and investment activity. This can be done on either the Goal (the same as the portfolio) or account level, depending on your preferences and any regulatory requirements. For Goals, you will need to depend on your own book of records because the custodian has no visibility of those. For accounts, you could just read a history of cash and investment transactions.

So, let's ignore the source for now and focus on the calculation. For P&L, we need three data points: a monetary valuation (of the account or Goal/portfolio), any new cash flows made prior to the value update, and a date associated with the value update:

```
history = pd.DataFrame(columns=['Date','Value','Cashflow'])
history = history.set_index('Date')
new_row = pd.Series({'Value':0,'Cashflow':0}, name=pd.
Timestamp('2019-12-30'))
history = history.append(new_row)
new_row = pd.Series({'Value':100000,'Cashflow': 100000},
name=pd.Timestamp('2019-12-31'))
history = history.append(new_row)
new_row = pd.Series({'Value':77985,'Cashflow':0}, name=pd.
Timestamp('2020-03-23'))
history = history.append(new_row)
new_row = pd.Series({'Value':110828,'Cashflow':0}, name=pd.
Timestamp('2020-12-31'))
history = history.append(new_row)
print(history)
```

This code will generate the following output:

```
              Value Cashflow
Date
2019-12-30        0        0
2019-12-31   100000   100000
2020-03-23    77985        0
2020-12-31   110828        0
```

We can then interpret the TWRR formula in terms of a Python function that loops through each period, multiplying the result of each:

```
def calculatePNL_TWRR(history: pd.DataFrame, annualized:
bool=False):
  twrr = 1.0
  beginValue = history.iloc[0]['Value']
  for period in range(len(history)-1):
    endValue = history.iloc[period+1]['Value']
    cashflow = history.iloc[period+1]['Cashflow']
    if beginValue > 0.0 or cashflow > 0.0:
      periodReturn = (endValue-(beginValue+cashflow))/
(beginValue+cashflow)
      twrr = (1+periodReturn)*twrr
    beginValue = endValue

  twrr = twrr - 1

  if annualized:
    from dateutil import parser
    startDateTime = history.iloc[0].name
    endDateTime = history.iloc[len(history)-1].name
    from dateutil.relativedelta import relativedelta
    delta = relativedelta(endDateTime, startDateTime)
    return pow((1+twrr),(365/(delta.days+(delta.years*365))))-1
  else:
    return twrr
```

When implementing this loop, we need to form the formula elements of beginning and end values by comparing consecutive dates (rows) in our transaction history. To avoid crashing our code by dividing by zero, we want to skip any periods with zero changes. Finally, we use the familiar `relativedelta` function, which calculates the time difference between two dates, to calculate an annualized return where necessary.

If we try our new function, it will generate the following output:

```
print(calculatePNL_TWRR(history=history))
0.10827999999999993
```

We can confirm that the function actually ignores cash flows by trying another example, with a withdrawal of $10,000 in the middle:

```
history = pd.DataFrame(columns=['Date','Value','Cashflow'])
history = history.set_index('Date')
new_row = pd.Series({'Value':0,'Cashflow':0}, name=pd.
Timestamp('2019-12-30'))
history = history.append(new_row)
new_row = pd.Series({'Value':100000,'Cashflow':100000},
name=pd.Timestamp('2019-12-31'))
history = history.append(new_row)
new_row = pd.Series({'Value':77985,'Cashflow':0}, name=pd.
Timestamp('2020-03-23'))
history = history.append(new_row)
new_row = pd.Series({'Value':67985,'Cashflow':-10000}, name=pd.
Timestamp('2020-03-23'))
history = history.append(new_row)
new_row = pd.Series({'Value':96616,'Cashflow':0}, name=pd.
Timestamp('2020-12-31'))
history = history.append(new_row)
```

Now, if you rerun the `calculatePNL_TWRR` call, you will see the result is still 10.8%.

```
print(calculatePNL_TWRR(history=history))
0.1082737015518127
```

That's all we need for P&L itself. However, just a number isn't always that powerful, so a visual point of reference is helpful. That's where a benchmark comes in.

Comparing portfolio performance to a benchmark

A benchmark is just a well-established point of reference. In the world of investments, that is usually the S&P 500 Index, which is reflected in the SPY ETF. So, let's find out how our portfolio compares.

If we pick up the previously useful `yfinance` module, we can retrieve some price history on SPY with just one line of code.

```
benchmarkTicker = "SPY"
data = yf.download(benchmarkTicker, group_by="Ticker",
period="5y")
data
```

You'll get an output that looks similar to this:

```
Open   High   Low   Close   Adj Close   Volume
Date
2017-12-01   264.760010   265.309998   260.760010
264.459991   242.683990   164390900
2017-12-04   266.309998   266.799988   264.079987
264.140015   242.390366   94040600
2017-12-05   263.190002   265.149994   263.040009
263.190002   241.518600   77994500
2017-12-06   263.299988   263.730011   262.709991
263.239990   241.564499   75898600
2017-12-07   264.070007   264.429993   262.940002
264.070007   242.326111   77218600

...   ...   ...   ...   ...   ...   ...
2022-11-23   399.549988   402.929993   399.309998
402.420013   402.420013   68261600
2022-11-25   401.829987   402.910004   401.540009
402.329987   402.329987   30545400
2022-11-28   399.089996   400.809998   395.109985
395.910004   395.910004   67881600
2022-11-29   396.049988   397.299988   393.299988
395.230011   395.230011   52310000
2022-11-30   395.489990   407.679993   393.480011
407.679993   407.679993   144264900
1258 rows × 6 columns
```

We'll use our previous DataFrame trickery to clean this up, using just the close prices as our reference:

```
data = data.iloc[:, data.columns.get_level_values(0)=="Close"]
data = data.rename(columns={"Close": benchmarkTicker})
data = data.dropna()
data
```

This will clean things up considerably, as shown here:

```
SPY
Date
2017-11-30  265.010010
2017-12-01  264.459991
2017-12-04  264.140015
2017-12-05  263.190002
2017-12-06  263.239990
...    ...
2022-11-22  399.899994
2022-11-23  402.420013
2022-11-25  402.329987
2022-11-28  395.910004
2022-11-29  395.230011
1258 rows × 1 columns
```

Since we're going to compare investment products, we should change these details to percentages, making them more friendly for visualization later:

```
data[benchmarkTicker] = 100*(data[benchmarkTicker] / data.
iloc[0][benchmarkTicker])-100
data
```

In the following output, you'll see the first value is a zero, and the rest are % changes above or below that:

```
SPY
Date
2017-11-30   0.000000
2017-12-01  -0.207546
2017-12-04  -0.328288
2017-12-05  -0.686769
2017-12-06  -0.667907
```

```
...    ...
2022-11-22   50.899958
2022-11-23   51.850873
2022-11-25   51.816902
2022-11-28   49.394358
2022-11-29   49.137767
1258 rows × 1 columns
```

This also makes P&L pretty obvious. Now, we can just stick this dataset into a plot and see what we get:

```
import matplotlib.pyplot as plt
plt.plot(data)
plt.show()
```

The output will be similar to the following:

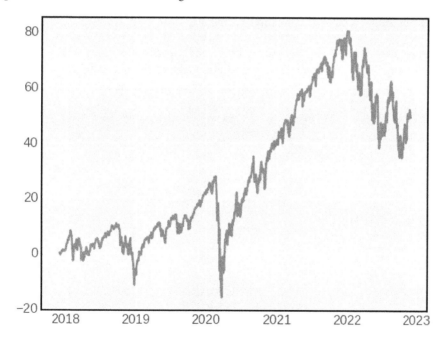

Figure 13.1 – An example performance chart for SPY

The impacts of the COVID-19 crash of 2020 and the recession fears of 2022 are strikingly clear in this chart. Now, we'll want to do the same for our portfolio. In this example, we're going to assume the benchmark makes sense in the context of our portfolio. You could, of course, do the same for the account level if you run a report from the custodian:

```
tickerString = ""
portfolio = myPortfolio
years=5


for allocation in portfolio.allocations:
  tickerString = tickerString + allocation.ticker + " "


data2 = yf.download(tickerString, group_by="Ticker",
period=str(years)+"y")
data2 = data2.iloc[:, data2.columns.get_level_
values(1)=="Close"]
data2 = data2.dropna()
data2.columns = data2.columns.droplevel(1)
```

The first thing we need is a list of tickers to feed into yfinance. We'll reuse our portfolio from the previous chapter. The other change needed is to sum together all the constituent products of the portfolio, multiplied by the allocation percentage. This then represents the total value of our portfolio at any given time:

```
for allocation in portfolio.allocations:
  data2[allocation.ticker] = data2[allocation.ticker] *
allocation.percentage
data2
```

The output will look as follows:

	DBC	IEI	TLT	VTI	GLD
Date					
2017-12-01	0.0	27.655214	8.880014	46.037926	44.472757
2017-12-04	0.0	27.634900	8.884224	45.977022	44.322797
2017-12-05	0.0	27.637157	8.928431	45.780785	44.008243
2017-12-06	0.0	27.668758	8.959306	45.753717	43.916803
2017-12-07	0.0	27.643929	8.889136	45.936423	43.338902
...	...	...	...	...	...
2022-11-23	0.0	26.021001	7.245052	68.138292	59.648141
2022-11-25	0.0	26.025517	7.220493	68.189041	59.699348
2022-11-28	0.0	26.027773	7.240842	67.082673	59.227514

```
2022-11-29  0.0  25.987143  7.155937  66.977789  59.520123
2022-11-30  0.0  26.163206  7.208564  69.041660  60.280905
1258 rows × 5 columns
```

We can see that the allocation for DBC is zero. Now, we can add these together and calculate the relative changes as before with SPY:

```
data2["Total"] = data2[list(data2.columns)].sum(axis=1)
data2["Portfolio"] = 100*(data2["Total"] / data2.iloc[0]
["Total"])-100
data2 = data2.filter(['Portfolio'])
data2
```

We only need the portfolio value, so we'll delete the other columns. The output will look as follows:

```
Portfolio
Date
2017-12-01    0.000000
2017-12-04   -0.178650
2017-12-05   -0.544130
2017-12-06   -0.588234
2017-12-07   -0.974074
...    . . .
2022-11-23   26.767156
2022-11-25   26.831630
2022-11-28   25.607193
2022-11-29   25.656143
2022-11-30   28.059482
1258 rows × 1 columns
```

Now, we can easily add this to the same chart as SPY:

```
plt.plot(data, label=benchmarkTicker)
plt.plot(data2, label="Portfolio")
plt.legend(loc="upper left")
plt.show()
```

To clarify which line is which, we add a legend. The output is shown in the following screenshot:

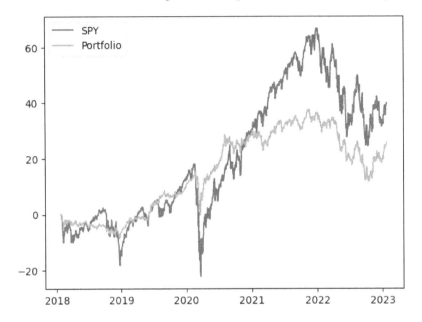

Figure 13.2 – Our example benchmark graph

One thing that stands out is that diversification works. While the overall performance of our portfolio is lower, the scares of 2019 and 2020 would have been much easier to stomach. This same chart could also be used for portfolio back-testing if that's something you wish to share with potential investors during the onboarding process. This allows investors to see how the portfolio would have reacted during key moments, starting from the 2008 global financial crisis to more recent events.

For completeness, let's go ahead and add our P&L calculation to the legend for ease of comparison. This is easy now:

```
profitBenchmark = data.iloc[len(data)-1][benchmarkTicker]/100
profitPortfolio = data2.iloc[len(data2)-1]["Portfolio"]/100
plt.plot(data, label=benchmarkTicker + ": " + '{0:.2f}'.
format(profitBenchmark*100) + "%")
plt.plot(data2, label="Portfolio: " + '{0:.2f}'.
format(profitPortfolio*100) + "%")
plt.legend(loc="upper left")
plt.show()
```

We will use some Python sorcery to just show two digits for our P&L results. The result looks like this:

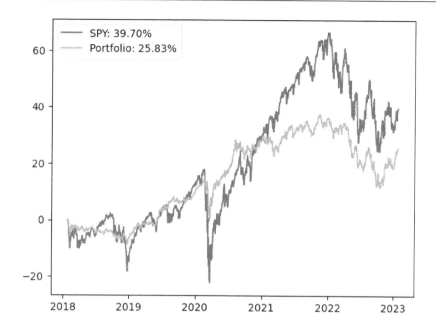

Figure 13.3 – Our complete benchmark chart with P&L

As before, we aren't done. Let's put everything we've learned together into a reusable function:

```
def benchmarkPortfolio(portfolio: Portfolio, benchmarkTicker:
str, years: int):
  import matplotlib.pyplot as plt
  data = yf.download(benchmarkTicker, group_by="Ticker",
    period=str(years)+"y")
  data = data.iloc[:, data.columns.get_level_
values(0)=="Close"]
  data = data.rename(columns={"Close": benchmarkTicker})
  data = data.dropna()
  data[benchmarkTicker] = 100*(data[benchmarkTicker] / data.
iloc[0][benchmarkTicker])-100
  tickerString=""
  for allocation in portfolio.allocations:
    tickerString = tickerString + allocation.ticker + " "
  data2 = yf.download(tickerString, group_by="Ticker",
    period=str(years)+"y")
  data2 = data2.iloc[:,
    data2.columns.get_level_values(1)=="Close"]
```

```
data2 = data2.dropna()
data2.columns = data2.columns.droplevel(1)
for allocation in portfolio.allocations:
    data2[allocation.ticker] = data2[allocation.ticker] *
data2["Total"] = data2[list(data2.columns)].sum(axis=1)
data2["Portfolio"] = 100*(
    data2["Total"] / data2.iloc[0] ["Total"])-100
data2 = data2.filter(['Portfolio'])
profitBenchmark = data.iloc[len(data)-1][benchmarkTicker]/100
profitPortfolio = data2.iloc[len(data2)-1]["Portfolio"]/100
plt.plot(data, label=benchmarkTicker + ": " + '{
    0:.2f}'.format(profitBenchmark*100) + "%")
plt.plot(data2, label="Portfolio: " + '{
    0:.2f}'.format(profitPortfolio*100) + "%")
plt.legend(loc="upper left")
plt.show()
```

Now, we have an easy one-line shortcut to do all that work for us, as follows:

```
benchmarkPortfolio(portfolio=myPortfolio,
benchmarkTicker="SPY", years=5)
```

We should see a very familiar output that matches *Figure 13.3* exactly. With these two functions, we can now easily calculate P&L and visualize a benchmark for our Goals.

Summary

This chapter gave us some important tools needed to track live Goals, portfolios, and accounts. We started by reviewing the two main methods for calculating P&L and choosing to focus on TWRR.

We tested a Python implementation of TWRR on a few examples, before moving on to benchmarking. There, we used the familiar yfinance module to retrieve price history data for the benchmark SPY ETF, as well as our portfolio. Step by step, we formatted our data to present it in a simple chart. Finally, we put together all our code into a reusable function.

The next chapter is going to be another exciting one, where we will discuss rebalancing. This functionality is often seen as the core of a Robo-advisor, so roll up your sleeves.

Rebalancing

In this chapter, we're going to implement a core capability for Robo-advisors in rebalancing. **Rebalancing** is the process of adjusting the allocation of assets in a portfolio to maintain the desired level of risk and return implied by the model portfolio. This involves selling some of the assets that have increased in value and buying more of the assets that have decreased in value, in order to bring the portfolio back to its original allocation.

Rebalancing can be done on a regular basis, such as quarterly or annually, or it can be done when the portfolio deviates from its target allocation by a certain amount, known as the **rebalancing threshold**.

Rebalancing is an important part of portfolio management, as it helps to maintain the desired level of risk and return, and to avoid concentration in a small number of assets. It also helps to capture the benefits of diversification, such as lower volatility and higher returns, and to reduce the impact of market fluctuations on the portfolio.

The first thing we'll do, hands-on, is calculate portfolio drift to see how far we are from the model portfolio, by checking the latest market prices. From there, we'll start with a basic implementation for time-based rebalancing, which will generate the expected buy and sell orders. Finally, we'll add a different trigger that compares drift to a set threshold.

In this chapter, we're going to cover the following topics:

- Calculating portfolio drift
- Implementing time-based rebalancing
- Implementing threshold-based rebalancing

Calculating portfolio drift

Portfolio drift is the gradual change in the allocation of assets in a portfolio over time. This can occur due to a number of factors, including changes in the market value of the assets.

Portfolio drift can have a number of negative effects on the portfolio, such as increased volatility, reduced diversification, and reduced returns. It can also cause the portfolio to deviate from its target allocation, which can affect an investor's ability to achieve their investment goals.

Let's look at how we can calculate portfolio drift:

1. First, we need to gather the current situation. We'll need to have the original model portfolio allocations, how many units we hold of each ETF, and the latest market prices for those ETFs:

```
allocations = [obj.percentage for obj in myPortfolio.
allocations]
holdings = [obj.units for obj in myPortfolio.allocations]
market_values = []
for allocation in myPortfolio.allocations:
  price = float(yf.Ticker(
    allocation.ticker).basic_info["previousClose"])
  market_values.append(price)
```

2. Now, we can calculate the implied allocations from the market prices:

```
current_allocation = []
for i in range(len(holdings)):
    current_allocation.append(
        holdings[i] * market_values[i])
current_allocation = [x / sum(current_allocation) for x
in current_allocation]
print(current_allocation)
```

You should see something like this:

```
[0.0, 0.08180071695955103, 0.20339845018629402,
0.37334092885284614, 0.34145990400130877]
```

3. Now, we can simply calculate the differences between this current allocation and the model portfolio allocation we want to maintain:

```
diff = [x1 - x2 for (x1, x2) in zip(
    allocations, current_allocation)]
print("Portfolio Drift: " + '{0:.2f}'.format((
    np.abs(diff).sum()/2)*100) + "%")
```

This is another useful Python shorthand for comparing two lists and their values. We then sum the absolute values of the differences and divide them by two. The output will be as follows:

```
Portfolio Drift: 2.23%
```

4. Let's put this together in a reusable function. This can be done separately or perhaps as a class method within the `Portfolio` class. That's what we'll do here:

```python
def calculateDrift(self) -> float:
    allocations = [
        obj.percentage for obj in self.allocations]
    holdings = [obj.units for obj in self.allocations]
    if sum(holdings) == 0.0:
        return -1
    market_values = []
    for allocation in self.allocations:
        price = float(yf.Ticker(
            allocation.ticker).basic_info["previousClose"])
        market_values.append(price)

    current_allocation = []
    for i in range(len(holdings)):
        current_allocation.append(
            holdings[i] * market_values[i])
    current_allocation = [x / sum(
        current_allocation) for x in current_allocation]

    diff = [x1 - x2 for (x1, x2) in zip(
        allocations, current_allocation)]
    return(np.abs(diff).sum()/2)
```

Remember that if you replace an earlier class, you'll now have to rerun the code in *Chapter 12* to end up with a myPortfolio object that actually has filled units. If you don't, either calling `calculateDrift()` will result in an error because it's not found, or if you create a new myPortfolio object with zero units, you will get a result of –1. If you did everything correctly, you should see the following output:

```
myPortfolio.calculateDrift()
0.02233083285415495
```

So, there we have it. Now, the question is what to do about this drift. The solution is rebalancing.

Implementing time-based rebalancing

The trigger for time-based rebalancing is just the calendar. Typical schemes might be annual – a specific date such as December 31, or quarterly, which might be set dates at the end of each quarter.

Before we get to the rebalancing algorithm, let's do a little cleanup to ensure we are reusing our code in the `Portfolio` class. Because we want to reuse those handy differences between the model and current allocations, let's separate that from our current drift function:

```python
def calculateDiffsToModel(self) -> list:
    allocations = [obj.percentage for obj in self.allocations]
    holdings = [obj.units for obj in self.allocations]
    if sum(holdings) == 0.0:
      return []
    market_values = []
    for allocation in self.allocations:
      price = float(yf.Ticker(
          allocation.ticker).basic_info["previousClose"])
      market_values.append(price)

    current_allocation = []
    for i in range(len(holdings)):
        current_allocation.append(
          holdings[i] * market_values[i])
    current_allocation = [x / sum(
        current_allocation) for x in current_allocation]

    diff = [x1 - x2 for (x1, x2) in zip(
        allocations, current_allocation)]
    return diff

def calculateDrift(self) -> float:
    diff = self.calculateDiffsToModel()
    return(np.abs(diff).sum()/2)
```

Now we have two class methods under the `Portfolio` class instead of one. Our `calculateDrift()` method seems incredibly simple now, as it uses the output of the other method, `calculateDiffsToModel()`. We also change the return value to an empty list if holdings are empty.

Thanks to all the work we completed in the previous chapter, rebalancing is simply a matter of generating the appropriate orders. Since we're not buying or selling entire portfolios, we can bypass the splitting engine and directly generate split orders for specific ETFs. Let's do this directly as another class method:

```python
def Rebalance(self) -> list:
    diff = self.calculateDiffsToModel()
    splitOrders = []
    for i in range(len(diff)):
        if diff[i] > 0:
            diffValue = diff[i] * holdings[i] *
            market_values[i]
            newOrder = Order(
                account = myAccount,
                goal = myGoal,
                transactionType = TransactionType('BUY'),
                dollarAmount = diffValue)
            splitOrders.append(SplitOrder(
                originalOrder = newOrder,
                ticker = myPortfolio.allocations[i].ticker,
                dollarAmount = diffValue))
        elif diff[i] < 0:
            diffValue = abs(diff[i]) * holdings[i] *
            market_values[i]
            newOrder = Order(
                account = myAccount,
                goal = myGoal,
                transactionType = TransactionType('SELL'),
                dollarAmount = diffValue)
            splitOrders.append(SplitOrder(
                originalOrder = newOrder,
                ticker = myPortfolio.allocations[i].ticker,
                dollarAmount = diffValue))
    return splitOrders
```

We reused the methods we created to get the information required to populate our `newOrder` and `SplitOrder` objects. Since we only check for differences above or below zero, we will automatically avoid creating orders where no drift exists. This can happen when there is no allocation of a specific product in the model portfolio. If we run this function, we can recover the orders created and print them out:

```
for split in splits:
    print(split.ticker + ": " + split.originalOrder.
transactionType.value + " " + '${0:.2f}'.format(split.
dollarAmount))
```

Your output will be something like the following:

```
TLT: BUY $0.02
IEI: BUY $0.01
GLD: SELL $0.06
VTI: SELL $0.02
```

For platforms with a high number of accounts, you would do this in batches. During that period – for example, 1–3 days, you might temporarily suspend other transactions for those accounts in the queue to avoid messing with the rebalancing calculations.

If instead, we wish to use a threshold trigger, we need some more logic.

Implement threshold-based rebalancing

To implement threshold-based rebalancing, we simply set a threshold for portfolio drift. To identify this, we can continue from our preceding example. First, we need a way to mark which portfolios require rebalancing. Let's add a Boolean flag to our Portfolio class from before:

```
class Portfolio:
    def __init__(self, tickerString: str, expectedReturn: float,
        portfolioName: str, riskBucket: int):
        self.name = portfolioName
        self.riskBucket = riskBucket
        self.expectedReturn = expectedReturn
        self.allocations = []
        self.needRebalancing = False
```

For the sake of brevity, I haven't added the full Portfolio class, so just add this line to the __init__() method.

Let's add a helper method to check whether our portfolio's drift is higher than the threshold:

```
def checkNeedRebalancing(self, thres: float, diff: list=[]):
    if diff == []:
```

```
    diff = self.calculateDiffsToModel()
  drift = self.calculateDrift(diff)

  if drift >= thres:
    self.needRebalancing = True
  else:
    self.needRebalancing = False
```

To avoid having to recalculate the differences, we can also refactor our previous methods to take in a list of differences provided by calculateDiffsToModel(). Then, we just set the flag to True if the threshold is crossed.

Now, we can loop through all portfolios and mark them with our handy function:

```
threshold = 0.1
accounts = [myAccount, myAccount2]
for account in accounts:
  for goal in account.goals:
    diffs = goal.portfolio.calculateDiffsToModel()
    goal.portfolio.checkNeedRebalancing(diff=diffs,
                                       thres=threshold)
```

We can now check the results:

```
print(myAccount.goals[0].portfolio.needRebalancing)
print(myAccount2.goals[0].portfolio.needRebalancing)
```

Depending on when you run this code, you may get either one as False or True; in my case, both were False.

Now, we need a minor modification of our rebalancing method to check this new flag:

```
def Rebalance(self, diff: list=[]) -> list:
    if diff == []:
      diff = self.calculateDiffsToModel()

    if not self.needRebalancing:
      return []

    splitOrders = []
    for I in range(len(diff)):
```

```
        if diff[i] > 0:
            diffValue = diff[i] * holdings[i] *
            market_values[i]
            newOrder = Order(
                account = myAccount,
                goal = myGoal,
                transactionType = TransactionType('BUY'),
                dollarAmount = diffValue)
            splitOrders.append(SplitOrder(
                originalOrder = newOrder,
                ticker = myPortfolio.allocations[i].ticker,
                dollarAmount = diffValue))
        elif diff[i] < 0:
            diffValue = abs(diff[i]) * holdings[i] *
            market_values[i]
            newOrder = Order(
                account = myAccount,
                goal = myGoal,
                transactionType = TransactionType('SELL'),
                dollarAmount = diffValue)
            splitOrders.append(SplitOrder(
                originalOrder = newOrder,
                ticker = myPortfolio.allocations[i].ticker,
                dollarAmount = diffValue))
    return splitOrders
```

Now, we can avoid unnecessary rebalancing. You can check portfolios on a daily basis, and then run rebalancing as a batch for any portfolio in need. Depending on your choice of threshold, this may trigger lots of orders in volatile markets, so take that into consideration.

Summary

In this chapter, we added the last major capability to our Robo-advisor – rebalancing. Rebalancing is the process of adjusting the allocation of assets in a portfolio to maintain the desired level of risk and return, and can be done on a regular basis or when the portfolio deviates from its target allocation. We established two main strategies for rebalancing – time-based and threshold-based.

We started off by looking at portfolio drift. This is the gradual change in the allocation of assets in a portfolio over time and can be addressed through regular rebalancing. Then, we added an implementation for time-based rebalancing, which gave us the reusable methods needed to generate orders for any portfolio. Finally, we added some tweaks that allowed us to set a threshold-based trigger to decide which portfolios should be rebalanced.

The only thing left for us now is to consider the impact of dividends and fees. We'll discuss them in the next chapter.

15

Dividends and Fee Management

In this chapter, we will explore two important batch processes for a Robo-advisor platform: processing dividends and calculating platform fees. We will begin by receiving a dividend payout file from the custodian and using it to allocate dividends to specific goals. This process will be designed to be run on a daily basis on the platform.

Next, we will focus on calculating platform fees using market data. We will then put all of these steps together into a reusable function that generates a CSV file that can be sent to the broker for execution.

By the end of this chapter, you will have a better understanding of how to implement these batch processes and how they can be used to support the operation of a Robo-advisor platform.

In this chapter, we're going to cover the following topics:

- Calculating dividends
- Calculating fees

Calculating dividends

A **dividend** is a payment made by a company to its shareholders, typically out of its profits or reserves. Dividends are a way for companies to distribute some of their earnings to shareholders and are typically paid in cash or additional shares of the company's stock. In our case, the ETFs within our portfolios are themselves composed of stocks that pay dividends.

Accumulation and income ETFs are both types of ETFs, which are investment vehicles that track a basket of underlying assets, such as stocks or bonds. The main difference between accumulation and income ETFs is the way that they distribute their earnings.

Accumulation ETFs, also known as **capitalization-weighted ETFs**, do not pay dividends to investors. Instead, they *accumulate* the dividends received from the underlying assets and reinvest them back into the fund. This means that the value of the fund's shares will increase over time as the dividends are reinvested and the fund's holdings appreciate in value.

Income ETFs, on the other hand, pay out the dividends received from the underlying assets to investors on a regular basis. This means that investors in an income ETF will receive regular cash payments in the form of dividends, but the value of the fund's shares may not increase as quickly as those of an accumulation ETF.

Typically, custodians would update you on any dividends received. So, let's assume you receive the following file that contains any new dividends per account. We have purposely omitted the rounding of units and amounts in this chapter, which is left to you to implement based on the specifications of your broker and custodian. This is crucial in order to prevent small fractional mismatches between the Robo-advisor and custodian.

	A	B	C	D
1	Account	Symbol	Amount	Units
2	123456789	TLT	0	0.0004871720117
3	123456789	IEI	0	0.0003595316567
4	123456789	VTI	0.1699714236	0
5	987654321	IEI	0	0.002256999133
6	987654321	VTI	0.1937368557	0

Figure 15.1 – Example of dividends received from the custodian

We will read the file:

```
newDividends = pd.read_csv('/content/Data/Dividends.csv')
print(newDividends)
```

We should see the following output:

```
   Account Symbol    Amount     Units
0  123456789    TLT  0.000000  0.000487
1  123456789    IEI  0.000000  0.000360
```

```
2    123456789     VTI    0.169971    0.000000
3    987654321     IEI    0.000000    0.002257
4    987654321     VTI    0.193737    0.000000
```

You'll notice that we have two columns with numbers. Some ETFs have no dividends, and some accumulate dividends, but the ones that pay out dividends can pay them out as new units or cash. In this example, we can imagine both and need to match these to any goals in those accounts listed. This is a very similar task to that which we tackled previously in *Chapter 12*.

We would want to run this process across all accounts on a daily basis, to check for any new dividends from the custodian and then allocate those across goals. Since we haven't created a database in our examples, I'm just going to start with a list of accounts. In reality, you would retrieve these from your database instead:

```
accounts = [myAccount, myAccount2]
```

Now, we want to start off by confirming the current situation before we process dividends:

```
for account in accounts:
  print("Account: " + str(account.number))
  print("Cash: " + str(account.cashBalance))
  for goal in account.goals:
    print("Portfolio: " + goal.portfolio.name)
    for allocation in goal.portfolio.allocations:
      print(allocation.ticker + ", units: " + str(
          allocation.units))
    print("\n")
```

This will produce the following output:

```
Account: 123456789
Cash: 1.035132710930999
Portfolio: Moderate
IEI, units: 0.017830019349873338
DBC, units: 0.0
TLT, units: 0.009743440233
GLD, units: 0.021787342483294347
VTI, units: 0.016623677770812747


Account: 987654321
```

```
Cash: 0.9648672844086992
Portfolio: Conservative
TLT, units: 0.0
IEI, units: 0.11299652015012668
DBC, units: 0.0
GLD, units: 0.019422680796705658
VTI, units: 0.01903574467918725
```

This gives us a baseline to compare to, so we can confirm that it worked. Now, we can proceed to process each line of the dividend updates we received in the CSV file from the custodian:

```python
for index, row in newDividends.iterrows():
  accountNo = row['Account']

  account = next((account for account in accounts if
str(account.number) == str(accountNo)), None)

  if account == None:
    print("No account")
    break

  if row['Amount'] > 0:
    account.cashBalance += row['Amount']
  elif row['Units'] > 0:
    unitsToAllocate = row['Units']
    unitsAcrossPortfolios = 0.0

    for goal in account.goals:
      for allocation in goal.portfolio.allocations:
        if allocation.ticker == row['Symbol']:
          unitsAcrossPortfolios += allocation.units

    for goal in account.goals:
      for allocation in goal.portfolio.allocations:
        if (allocation.ticker == row['Symbol']) and
(unitsAcrossPortfolios > 0):
          allocation.units += unitsToAllocate * (allocation.
units / unitsAcrossPortfolios)
```

To find the `Account` object that matches the line in our CSV file, we use the `next()` method, which returns a default value of `None` if nothing matches. If the dividend is paid in cash, we simply update the account balance accordingly. While this isn't optimal for large numbers of dividends or accounts, we use two sequential `for` loops to first count the total units for each symbol found in the account, and then update the units pro rata.

Once that code is executed, we can re-run our `print` statements to see what happened:

```
for account in accounts:
  print("Account: " + str(account.number))
  print("Cash: " + str(account.cashBalance))
  for goal in account.goals:
    print("Portfolio: " + goal.portfolio.name)
    for allocation in goal.portfolio.allocations:
      print(allocation.ticker + ", units: " + str(allocation.
units))
    print("\n")
```

You should now see updated cash balances and units. Note that the file did not include dividends for all symbols in the portfolio, as some ETFs do not pay out dividends. Further, different ETFs would pay out their dividends at different times and frequencies:

```
Account: 123456789
Cash: 1.205104134530999
Portfolio: Moderate
IEI, units: 0.018189551006573337
DBC, units: 0.0
TLT, units: 0.0102306122447
GLD, units: 0.021787342483294347
VTI, units: 0.016623677770812747

Account: 987654321
Cash: 1.1586041401086993
Portfolio: Conservative
TLT, units: 0.0
IEI, units: 0.11525351928312667
DBC, units: 0.0
GLD, units: 0.019422680796705658
VTI, units: 0.01903574467918725
```

That does the job. Now, we can just clean this up by creating a reusable method, which could be a scheduled batch run each day once the custodian has updated their **Start Of Day (SOD)** files:

```python
def allocateDividends(dividendFile: pd.DataFrame, accounts:
list):

  for index, row in dividendFile.iterrows():
    accountNo = row['Account']

    account = next((account for account in accounts if
str(account.number) == str(accountNo)), None)

    if account == None:
      print("No account")
      break

    if row['Amount'] > 0:
      account.cashBalance += row['Amount']
    elif row['Units'] > 0:
      unitsToAllocate = row['Units']
      unitsAcrossPortfolios = 0.0

      for goal in account.goals:
        for allocation in goal.portfolio.allocations:
          if allocation.ticker == row['Symbol']:
            unitsAcrossPortfolios += allocation.units

      for goal in account.goals:
        for allocation in goal.portfolio.allocations:
          if allocation.ticker == row['Symbol']:
            allocation.units += unitsToAllocate * (allocation.
units / unitsAcrossPortfolios)
```

The only difference here is that now, we pass the dividend file and accounts list to the function.

If you need to update the investor that their accounts have received new dividends, then you need more information than the custodian has shared. Luckily, the trusty `yfinance` Python module has us covered once again. We can find the dividend schedule for any instrument as follows:

```
spy = yf.Ticker("SPY")
spy.dividend
```

You'll see a printout like so:

```
Date
1993-03-19 00:00:00-05:00      0.213
1993-06-18 00:00:00-04:00      0.318
1993-09-17 00:00:00-04:00      0.286
1993-12-17 00:00:00-05:00      0.317
1994-03-18 00:00:00-05:00      0.271
                               ...
2021-09-17 00:00:00-04:00      1.428
2021-12-17 00:00:00-05:00      1.633
2022-03-18 00:00:00-04:00      1.366
2022-06-17 00:00:00-04:00      1.577
2022-09-16 00:00:00-04:00      1.596
Name: Dividends, Length: 120, dtype: float64
```

This gives us the dividend date and the dividend amount per share. If needed, you could provide this information both retroactively to highlight when dividends are paid, and when future dividends are due. To clarify, these dates are ex-dividend dates, which are when the dividend amounts are determined by the custodian. The actual payment dates may be different, typically 1-2 weeks later.

If you just want to show the current dividend yield, you can get that through the `info` dictionary property:

```
Spy.info['yield']
0.016
```

That gives us the basic building blocks needed to process dividends. Now, we can move on to fee management.

Calculating fees

For the sake of simplicity, we have so far largely ignored fees. In a Robo-advisor, there are many levels and sources of potential fees. Fees will be imposed on your platform by all providers: broker, custodian, payment gateway(s), market data feed(s), and cloud hosting.

At the end of the day, it is up to you how you wish to pass those costs to your own customers, and how you wish to structure those fees. Some fees will be volume-based, such as transaction fees by the broker, or infrastructure consumption from cloud hosting. Others will be fixed in nature. How much you will need to charge your customers is an exercise left for you.

Generally, there are two broad fee mechanisms applied by Robo-advisors to their customers: subscriptions and **Assets Under Management** (**AUM**) fees. The latter is the more conventional approach and makes it easy for investors to compare AUM fees charged by other providers, such as mutual fund providers, hedge funds, and financial advisors. Some have opted for subscriptions more in the vein of a Netflix or Spotify model. These fees can be tiered to offer different levels of product access and support.

For the sake of this exercise, we'll look at an example of calculating AUM fees. AUM fees are fees charged by investment managers based on the total assets under their management. These fees are typically calculated as a percentage of the AUM and are used to compensate the investment manager for their services.

For example, an investment manager might charge a 1% AUM fee for managing a portfolio of $1 million. In this case, the investment manager would receive $10,000 in annualized AUM fees ($1 million x 1%) for managing the portfolio.

AUM fees are commonly used by investment managers because they align the interests of the manager and the investor. The investment manager is incentivized to maximize the value of the assets under their management because this will increase the AUM fees that they receive. At the same time, the investor benefits from the investment manager's efforts to grow the value of the assets, as a larger portfolio will generate higher AUM fees for the manager.

As we did with dividends, we will start with the same list of accounts:

```
accounts = [myAccount, myAccount2]
```

Now, we can use the same methods we used for dividends to run through the accounts and goals to find out how much AUM each account has today:

```
for account in accounts:
  print("Account: " + str(account.number))
  print("Cash: " + str(account.cashBalance))
  aum = 0.0
  for goal in account.goals:
    print("Portfolio: " + goal.portfolio.name)
    for allocation in goal.portfolio.allocations:
      price = float(yf.Ticker(
          allocation.ticker).basic_info["previousClose"])
```

```
        aum += price * allocation.units
    print("AUM: " + '${0:.2f}'.format(aum))
    print("\n")
```

We use yfinance yet again to get our prices for the last close. The output should be like so:

```
Account: 123456789
Cash: 1.3350306235113794
Portfolio: Moderate
AUM: $10.12


Account: 987654321
Cash: 1.028677651128318
Portfolio: Conservative
AUM: $20.69
```

That's well and good, but to calculate fees, we need to find the average AUM over the fee period. If we assume we're charging fees on a monthly basis, that would last month. So, we need to find daily prices for that period. Let's start by capturing all the ETFs in our accounts:

```
tickerString = ""
for account in accounts:
    for goal in account.goals:
        for allocation in goal.portfolio.allocations:
            if not allocation.ticker in tickerString:
                tickerString += allocation.ticker + " "
print(tickerString)
> IEI TLT DBC GLD VTI
```

Now, we can move on to finding out last month's dates:

```
from datetime import datetime, timedelta
from calendar import monthrange
today = datetime.today()
first_day_of_month = today.replace(day=1)
_, num_days_in_prev_month = monthrange(first_day_of_month.year,
first_day_of_month.month-1)
first_day_of_prev_month = first_day_of_month -
timedelta(days=num_days_in_prev_month)
last_day_of_prev_month = first_day_of_month - timedelta(days=1)
```

These utility functions give us everything we need. We get the last day by starting from the first day of this month and going back one day. Now, we're ready to retrieve our price data all at once:

```
data = yf.download(tickerString, group_by="Ticker",
start=first_day_of_prev_month, end=last_day_of_prev_month)
data = data.iloc[:, data.columns.get_level_values(1)=="Close"]
data = data.dropna()
data.columns = data.columns.droplevel(1)
data
```

We added in our usual DataFrame formatting to end up with a clean result. It should look like this:

Date	IEI	TLT	DBC	GLD	VTI
2022-11-01	113.209999	96.769997	25.500000	153.460007	193.429993
2022-11-02	113.110001	96.349998	25.730000	152.389999	188.339996
2022-11-03	112.750000	95.830002	25.709999	151.809998	186.539993
2022-11-04	112.839996	94.220001	26.580000	156.470001	188.940002
2022-11-07	112.610001	93.279999	26.350000	155.850006	190.660004
2022-11-08	113.010002	94.300003	26.030001	159.449997	191.660004
2022-11-09	113.360001	94.610001	25.430000	158.649994	187.529999
2022-11-10	114.989998	98.250000	25.660000	163.479996	198.139999
2022-11-11	114.849998	97.889999	26.150000	164.559998	200.160004
2022-11-14	114.669998	97.650002	25.760000	164.919998	198.350006
2022-11-15	115.180000	99.230003	26.059999	165.500000	200.360001
2022-11-16	115.529999	101.400002	25.770000	165.119995	198.320007
2022-11-17	115.070000	100.330002	25.340000	163.919998	197.490005
2022-11-18	114.769997	99.639999	25.160000	162.789993	198.419998
2022-11-21	114.730003	100.059998	25.070000	161.880005	197.580002
2022-11-22	114.940002	101.480003	25.330000	162.070007	200.169998
2022-11-23	115.279999	103.250000	24.980000	163.080002	201.389999
2022-11-25	115.300003	102.900002	24.760000	163.220001	201.539993
2022-11-28	115.309998	103.190002	24.610001	161.929993	198.270004
2022-11-29	115.129997	101.980003	24.930000	162.729996	197.960007
2022-11-30	115.910004	102.730003	25.490000	164.809998	204.059998

Figure 15.2 – Daily price history for our portfolio last month

Now, we can modify our previous code to calculate the average daily AUM instead of today's AUM:

```
for account in accounts:
  print("Account: " + str(account.number))
  print("Cash: " + str(account.cashBalance))
  aum = 0.0
  for goal in account.goals:
    print("Portfolio: " + goal.portfolio.name)
```

```
    for allocation in goal.portfolio.allocations:
        for index, row in data.iterrows():
            price = row[allocation.ticker]
            aum += price * allocation.units
    aum = aum / len(data)
    print("Average AUM: " + '${0:.2f}'.format(aum))
    print("\n")
```

We add together the AUM number for each trading day in the month, and then divide the final number by the number of trading days in the month. The result is as follows:

```
Account: 123456789
Cash: 1.3350306235113794
Portfolio: Moderate
Average AUM: $9.73


Account: 987654321
Cash: 1.028677651128318
Portfolio: Conservative
Average AUM: $20.17
```

You can see that the numbers are now slightly different. Now, we're ready to calculate a fee! We'll keep using this same loop again. Let's assume a 10 **basis points (bps)** fee, which is a 10th of 1%:

```
feeRate = 0.001
for account in accounts:
    print("Account: " + str(account.number))
    print("Cash: " + str(account.cashBalance))
    aum = 0.0
    for goal in account.goals:
        print("Portfolio: " + goal.portfolio.name)
        for allocation in goal.portfolio.allocations:
            for index, row in data.iterrows():
                price = row[allocation.ticker]
                aum += price * allocation.units
    aum = aum / len(data)
    fee = aum * feeRate * (num_days_in_prev_month / 365)
    print("Average AUM: " + '${0:.2f}'.format(aum))
```

```
print("Fee: $" + str(fee))
print("\n")
```

You should see something like this:

```
Account: 123456789
Cash: 1.3350306235113794
Portfolio: Moderate
Average AUM: $9.73
Fee: $0.0007996344333910244


Account: 987654321
Cash: 1.028677651128318
Portfolio: Conservative
Average AUM: $20.17
Fee: $0.001658052571063181
```

As you can see, the fees in our scenario are extremely small, much less than one cent per account, so you might choose to wait until it rounds down to at least one cent before charging the fee. Another point to note here is that, in some cases, there may not be enough cash in the account to actually pay the fees. In that scenario, you will need to force a sell order for a small slice of the holdings of that account to pay for the fees. We'll leave that to you to add.

Now, we can put together a fee file that we would send to the broker to deduct from the accounts and deposit to our platform account:

```
feeRate = 0.001 # 10bps
feeTable = pd.DataFrame(columns=['Account','FeeAmount'])


for account in accounts:
  aum = 0.0
  for goal in account.goals:
    for allocation in goal.portfolio.allocations:
      for index, row in data.iterrows():
        price = row[allocation.ticker]
        aum += price * allocation.units
  aum = aum / len(data)
  fee = aum * feeRate * (num_days_in_prev_month / 365)
  new_row = {'Account':account.number, 'FeeAmount':fee}
```

```
feeTable = feeTable.append(new_row, ignore_index=True)
```

```
print(feeTable)
>     Account   FeeAmount
0   123456789    0.000800
1   987654321    0.001658
```

Because our fees are so minute, you can actually see that pandas has formatted them to a lower precision. Don't worry, the full number is still there, but it just doesn't show them unless you request the number in that cell. Meanwhile, we can also override this setting:

```
pd.set_option("display.precision", 8)
```

Now, if you re-run that code, you should see something like this:

```
      Account    FeeAmount
0   123456789   0.00079963
1   987654321   0.00165805
```

Before we send this file to the broker, let's go ahead and clean this all up into a reusable function as always:

```
def generateFeeInstructions(accounts: list) -> pd.DataFrame:
  tickerString = ""
  for account in accounts:
    for goal in account.goals:
      for allocation in goal.portfolio.allocations:
        if not allocation.ticker in tickerString:
          tickerString += allocation.ticker + " "

  from datetime import datetime, timedelta
  from calendar import monthrange
  today = datetime.today()
  first_day_of_month = today.replace(day=1)
  _, num_days_in_prev_month = monthrange(first_day_of_month.
year, first_day_of_month.month-1)
  first_day_of_prev_month = first_day_of_month -
timedelta(days=num_days_in_prev_month)
  last_day_of_prev_month = first_day_of_month -
timedelta(days=1)
```

```
  data = yf.download(tickerString, group_by="Ticker",
start=first_day_of_prev_month, end=last_day_of_prev_month)
  data = data.iloc[:, data.columns.get_level_
values(1)=="Close"]
  data = data.dropna()
  data.columns = data.columns.droplevel(1)


  feeRate = 0.001 # 10bps
  feeTable = pd.DataFrame(columns=['Account','FeeAmount'])


  for account in accounts:
    aum = 0.0
    for goal in account.goals:
      for allocation in goal.portfolio.allocations:
        for index, row in data.iterrows():
          price = row[allocation.ticker]
          aum += price * allocation.units
    aum = aum / len(data)
    fee = aum * feeRate * (num_days_in_prev_month / 365)
    new_row = {'Account':account.number, 'FeeAmount':fee}
    feeTable = feeTable.append(new_row, ignore_index=True)


  return feeTable
```

That's better. Now, we can save this file as a CSV to ship to the broker:

```
feeFile = generateFeeInstructions(accounts)
feeFile.to_csv('/content/Data/Fees.csv')
```

You should find something like this in your Google Drive folder:

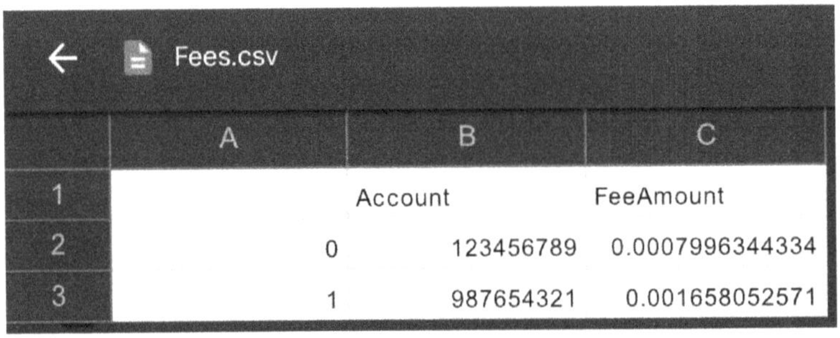

	A	B	C
1		Account	FeeAmount
2	0	123456789	0.0007996344334
3	1	987654321	0.001658052571

Figure 15.3 – Fee file generated for the broker

Well, if you made it this far, I want to congratulate you. You've just built yourself a Robo-advisor! Okay, maybe it's not ready to launch quite yet, but you've got all the basic building blocks figured out. Depending on your business plan, you may need to revisit *Chapters 3* and *4*.

Even if you're creating a prototype system, you'd want to create a database to persist all your data. However, the largest task ahead for you is to connect to your broker and custodian, and potentially, add a payment gateway provider. That should keep you busy for a while but do come back whenever you need a helpful reference.

Summary

In this chapter, we rounded out our suite of Robo-advisor capabilities by adding batch processes for dividends and fees. We started with processing dividends. First, we received a dividend payout file from the custodian. We ran through that file using pandas to extract which dividends should be allocated to which goals. This turned out as a reusable function that can be scheduled to run on a daily basis on your platform.

The second part of the chapter talked about fees. We focused on a scenario of calculating monthly platform AUM fees that we could send to the broker to extract on our behalf. We started off by calculating today's AUM, and then expanded that to cover the average daily AUM for the last month using market data from `yfinance`. Finally, we calculated fees using a 10 bps AUM fee. We put all this together into a reusable function that generates a CSV file that could be sent to the broker to execute on.

The final chapter of this book will discuss the impact of regulations on Robo-advisors, which may affect how you go about your plans from here.

Regulations for Robo-Advisors

In this chapter, we'll bring our journey together to a close by addressing a crucial topic for anyone interested in building and operating a Robo-advisor in regulations. This issue has been an area of active development since the global financial crisis of 2008 and the launch of the first Robo-advisors soon thereafter. Regulators wish to see Robo-advisors contributing positively to the financial services industry by using the opportunities offered by a digital experience to further investor protections and increase transparency on pricing. The issues are certainly made more challenging by the diversity of regulations and dynamics of capital markets around the world. In this chapter, we will attempt to give you an overview of the landscape.

We will begin this examination by breaking down some key themes around regulations that apply to Robo-advisors universally. From there, we will take a look at some key regulatory guidelines that have been set by authorities in America, the European Union, and Singapore. We'll cover the main licensing schemes that apply to Robo-advisors – both **Business-to-Consumer** (**B2C**) and **Business-to-Business** (**B2B**). The chapter ends with a comparison of how such licensing schemes may impact the capabilities and client experience of a Robo-advisor.

By the end of this chapter, you will have a better understanding of how regulations may apply to your plans for the operation of a Robo-advisor platform.

In this chapter, we're going to cover the following topics:

- Regulatory requirements to run your own Robo-advisor
- The differences between self-directed and managed portfolios

> **Important Note**
> None of the content in this chapter should be taken as legal advice. Regulations and guidelines are always subject to change; therefore, always seek local counsel to ensure compliance.

Regulatory requirements to run your own Robo-advisor

Generally, any type of Robo-advisor will be subject to rules, regulations, and guidelines set for financial services by local regulatory authorities. These guidelines may directly dictate the rules and boundaries for operating a Robo-advisor, or more often, for the broader class of *digital advice* services. Here are some typical items set out by such guidelines:

- **Licensing types**: The key question for most regulators is how Robo-advisors should be licensed, as that determines the exact requirements and reporting that such platforms must comply with. This question is not always black and white, as multiple licensing schemes may apply depending on the exact scenario each Robo-advisor is targeting with their business model.

- **Advisory process**: In certain countries, the level of detail of guidelines may include specific steps that should be followed while onboarding new clients. The intention is to ensure that such platforms comply with the basic requirements of what constitutes digital advice. This may cover steps such as risk profiling, portfolio selection, order management, and rebalancing.

- **Suitability**: One of the key considerations for Robo-advisor regulations is how recommendations are made. For example, how did a client end up with an aggressive portfolio for their retirement plan? There must be a way to track and report on such paths of actions and logic, ensuring that no investor can accidentally or incorrectly end up with an investment that would not be considered suitable given their circumstances. Documenting such circumstances, including employment status, financial standing, and salary information, may be part of such suitability requirements.

- **Anti-money laundering**: One of the financial services industry's greatest challenges in digitization has been to identify cases of potential impersonation or false identity that enable bad actors to participate in financial services. These risks include money laundering but also terrorism financing. A whole host of local laws and guidelines may apply here.

- **Algorithms**: Given the excitement around artificial intelligence and machine learning, many financial services technology companies have adopted these methods to offer novel capabilities to their clients. While such tools are not explicitly forbidden for Robo-advisors, guidelines may involve key decisions and recommendations around risk scoring, portfolio modeling, and selection. Given the pervasive trends, these may be subject to future revision.

In most countries, there are rules set by one or more authorities. Let's review some of the most important guidelines around the world.

Guidelines for Robo-advisors in America

The regulations for Robo-advisors vary, depending on the country and jurisdiction in which they operate. In the United States, for example, all Robo-advisors are subject to regulations from the **Securities and Exchange Commission** (**SEC**) and as broker-dealers under the **Financial Industry Regulatory Authority** (**FINRA**), where necessary.

The SEC's regulations for Robo-advisors include the Investment Advisers Act of 1940, which requires investment advisers to register with the SEC and maintain certain standards of conduct (SEC, 1940). The SEC also has specific rules for Robo-advisors that provide automated investment advice, such as disclosure requirements, risk questionnaires, and compliance processes (SEC, 2017). The SEC has already charged and fined several Robo-advisors for not being compliant with such guidelines (SEC, 2018).

FINRA has issued its own report on digital advice, which includes guidelines and best practices that cover specific issues around core capabilities, such as investor profiling, portfolios, rebalancing, and the use of algorithms (FINRA, 2016).

Guidelines for Robo-advisors in Europe

At the time of writing, the **European Union** (**EU**) does not have specific regulations governing the operation of Robo-advisors. However, Robo-advisors in the EU are subject to the same general regulations that apply to other financial services providers, such as investment firms and banks. Like America, the **European Securities and Markets Authority** (**ESMA**) has issued its own guidelines that touch on Robo-advisors, concerning existing key directives that echo themes around suitability in particular (ESMA, 2018).

The **European Parliament** (**EP**) has also created a study that provides an overview of relevant EU regulations and guidelines for Robo-advisors across various directive programs (EP 2021). The main piece of legislation that applies to Robo-advisors in the EU is the **Markets in Financial Instruments Directive** (**MiFID II**), which sets out rules for the conduct of investment firms and other financial services providers. Among other things, MiFID II requires investment firms to have systems and controls in place to manage the risks associated with their activities, and to ensure that they provide appropriate information to their clients (MiFID, 2014). These rules may apply to Robo-advisors operating inside EU jurisdiction, both in the capacity of investment advice and portfolio management. Considerations around algorithmic trading and the use of AI technologies by Robo-advisors are an area of ongoing scrutiny and likely further regulation.

For any platform operating in Europe, you will also need to consider **General Data Protection Regulation** (**GDPR**). The GDPR is a comprehensive data protection law that was adopted by the EU in 2016. The GDPR replaces the EU's previous data protection framework and establishes a new set of rules and standards for the collection, use, and storage of personal data. The GDPR applies to all organizations that handle the personal data of EU residents, regardless of where the organization is located, and imposes strict requirements on how personal data must be collected, used, and protected. The GDPR also gives individuals new rights and controls over their personal data, including the right to access, rectify, erase, and restrict the processing of their personal data. Overall, the GDPR is intended to provide greater protection for the personal data of EU residents, and to ensure that organizations handle personal data in a responsible and transparent manner.

Guidelines for Robo-advisors in Asia

In Asia, regulatory guidelines for Robo-advisors have been issued by the **Monetary Authority of Singapore (MAS)** for Singapore, as well as similar regulatory bodies in Hong Kong. The MAS issued its own guidelines for Robo-advisors in 2018 (MAS 2018). First and foremost, the MAS wanted to clarify its stance on the licensing requirements for Robo-advisors. This includes the need or exemption for either a financial advisory or **Capital Markets Services (CMS)** license. Here is an example from MAS on how to decide on applicable licensing for your Robo-advisor.

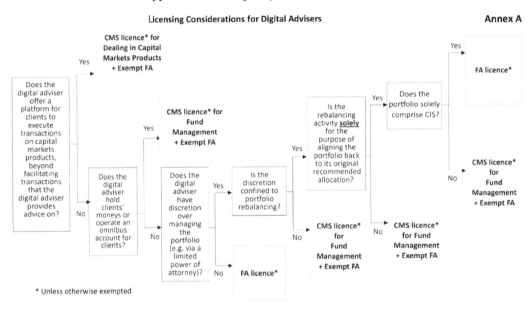

Figure 16.1: Licensing considerations for digital advisors (MAS 2018)

This diagram highlights the key considerations in licensing, which we will discuss in the following sections. In the MAS guidelines, a Robo-advisor that solely manages discretionary investments for the purposes of rebalancing to a model portfolio made of ETFs (or similar collective investment schemes) can be exempt from the much more stringent CMS regulations typically reserved for brokers. Another important piece of guidance was a partial exemption for Robo-advisors from needing to ask clients the full set of questions designed to prevent undue influence by human financial advisors, thus highlighting one of the great benefits of Robo-advisors for increased investor protection and suitability. The MAS guidelines have since been largely echoed across the region in similar publications by other regulators.

Licensing options for Robo-advisors – Investment advice versus portfolio management

There are several licensing options that may be available for Robo-advisors, depending on the specific services they offer and the regulatory environment in which they operate. In general, Robo-advisors can be licensed to provide strict investment advice or operate in the capital markets as a fund or portfolio manager. The Singapore guidelines in the previous section are an example of this distinction, just using local terminology instead of financial advisory or CMS.

Investment advice licensing is typically required for Robo-advisors that provide personalized investment recommendations to clients based on their specific financial goals and circumstances. In many jurisdictions, investment advice licensing may require Robo-advisors to meet certain requirements, such as having qualified staff, reporting, and insurance. For a Goal-based Robo-advisor, this would be the default approach for licensing. Generally, the requirements would be much easier to fulfill than a full portfolio manager license.

Portfolio management licensing is typically required for Robo-advisors that operate as brokers or dealers, and are involved in buying and selling securities and/or managing discretionary portfolios or investment mandates on behalf of clients. In many jurisdictions, portfolio licensing is regulated by securities regulators and may require Robo-advisors to meet much higher requirements than investment advice, such as more extensive compliance processes and reporting, and maintaining adequate capital reserves.

Either way, there are common requirements around staff experience; in particular, the C-level suite must have sufficient prior experience operating in financial services. In either licensing scheme, beyond your team's own compliance needs, you will have regulatory reporting duties that need to be handled by appropriate staff.

All of this as a whole means that most Robo-advisors aren't the result of dorm-room hacks by undergrads, and they tend to feature more of a seasoned founding team with the right kind of background to operate a regulated financial platform. The process and timeline of seeking appropriate licensing is something to consider carefully, as this cannot be fast-tracked as easily.

Licensing exemptions for B2B Robo-advisors

One important point to note is that thus far, B2B platforms have been exempt from licensing requirements. Such B2B Robo-advisors are seen as technology vendors; therefore, the company using said technology is the one subject to regulations. There are still several indirect regulations that do apply to even B2B platforms, the main one being **Technology Risk Management** (**TRM**). This outlines the dependencies and risks to the regulated company by using third-party technologies.

To ensure compliance with these TRM guidelines, many platforms seek certifications such as **Service Organization Control Type 2 (SOC2)**, which is a voluntary security-focused compliance standard for service organizations, developed by the **American Institute of CPA (AICPA)**. SOC2 is based on the following criteria: security, availability, processing integrity, confidentiality, and privacy.

Differences between self-directed and managed portfolios

Self-directed portfolios and managed portfolios are two different types of investment offerings that can be offered by Robo-advisors. While both types of portfolios may use similar investment strategies and tools, there are some key differences between them.

Self-directed portfolios are portfolios that are managed by an individual investor, rather than by a professional investment manager. In a self-directed portfolio, the investor has full control over which investments are included in the portfolio and is responsible for making all decisions about buying and selling securities. Self-directed portfolios may be suitable for investors who have a strong understanding of the financial markets and are comfortable making their own investment decisions.

Managed portfolios, on the other hand, are portfolios that are managed by a professional investment manager, such as a Robo-advisor. In a managed portfolio, the investment manager is responsible for making decisions about which investments to include in the portfolio, and for buying and selling securities on behalf of the investor. Managed portfolios may be suitable for investors who prefer to have a professional manage their investments, or who do not have the time or expertise to manage their own portfolios.

Requirements for a Robo-advisor platform with managed portfolios

Throughout this book, we have been using the approach of managed portfolios. Therefore, we have incorporated a process of having investors complete a risk questionnaire that is then mapped to a series of model portfolios via a fixed relationship. You can review that section of the book in *Chapter 8* and *Chapter 9*. This approach is generally associated with Robo-advisors offering services to retail investors, as it offers relatively little freedom to make extremely risky investments without advanced knowledge of doing so. Regulators view the mapping of risk scores to model portfolios as a safety feature, assuming the contents are following local guidelines. Many countries mandate specific questions to be included in the risk questionnaire, and the makeup and rationale for the construction of your model portfolios may be subject to regulatory approval.

Requirements for a Robo-advisor platform with self-directed portfolios

Depending on several factors relating to the intended audience, local regulations, and available licensing schemes, you may decide to opt for a different approach. With self-directed portfolios, most of the decision-making is left to the individual investor.

Rather than follow the flow we've established in this book for managed portfolios, you may not always need an explicit risk questionnaire at all. Investors may have the option to simply choose a risk profile based on a description and associated metrics for risk and returns. That choice may or may not correspond with a recommendation or choice of model portfolios. Some platforms may enable investors to either customize model portfolios or construct individualized portfolios entirely from scratch using their own preferences. Naturally, this path is far more suitable for experienced investors with knowledge of portfolio construction and risk modeling.

Note that the two models aren't necessarily mutually exclusive. For example, you may have Robo-advisors that not only offer standard managed portfolios as the baseline product, but also offer the option to either customize those portfolios or trade individual stocks or ETFs outside those portfolios. Of course, this type of intermingling may complicate matters behind the scenes. You may be required to set up separate accounts to keep portfolios and stock trading from crossing over, leading to different reporting requirements.

At the end of the day, all this comes down to your business plan and which path suits you best. This choice is closely tied to which licensing scheme will apply to your business. In certain cases, you will need several types of licensing to cover the types of financial services and products on offer.

Summary

We started this final chapter together by breaking down some key themes around regulations that apply to Robo-advisors universally. From there, we reviewed some key regulatory guidelines set by the authorities in America, the EU, and Singapore. We covered the main licensing schemes that apply to Robo-advisors, both B2C and B2B. The chapter ended with a comparison of how such licensing schemes may impact the capabilities and client experience of a Robo-advisor.

While this chapter is just a summary and not a comprehensive description of relevant regulations, it should help guide you on the right path. As stated at the beginning, nothing in this chapter should be taken as legal advice, so it's best to seek out local expertise and counsel where appropriate.

This is the end. You've made it! I trust you've enjoyed our journey together, and that you'll be able to put into practice many of the things we've learned along the way.

Further reading

You might be interested in reading some extra information related to the topics discussed in this chapter. Here are a few links to some of the external resources:

- SEC 1940. Investment Advisers Act of 1940. Accessed online 10.12.2022: `https://www.sec.gov/about/laws/iaa40.pdf`.

- SEC 2017. Guidance Update FEBRUARY 2017. Accessed online 10.12.2022: `https://www.sec.gov/investment/im-guidance-2017-02.pdf`.

- SEC 2018. SEC Charges Two Robo-Advisers With False Disclosures. Accessed online 10.12.2022: `https://www.sec.gov/news/press-release/2018-300`.

- FINRA 2016. Report on Digital Investment Advice March 2016. Accessed online 10.12.2022: `https://www.finra.org/sites/default/files/digital-investment-advice-report.pdf`.

- ESMA 2018. Guidelines on certain aspects of the MiFID II suitability requirements. Accessed online 10.12.2022: `https://www.esma.europa.eu/sites/default/files/library/esma35-43-1163_guidelines_on_certain_aspects_of_mifid_ii_suitability_requirements_0.pdf`.

- EP 2021. Robo-advisors, How do they fit in the existing EU regulatory framework, in particular with regard to investor protection? Accessed online 10.12.2022: `https://www.europarl.europa.eu/RegData/etudes/STUD/2021/662928/IPOL_STU(2021)662928_EN.pdf`

- MIFID 2014. Directive 2014/65/EU. Accessed online 10.12.2022: `https://eur-lex.europa.eu/legal-content/en/TXT/?uri=CELEX:32014L0065`.

- MAS 2018. Guidelines On Provision Of Digital Advisory Services. Accessed online 10.12.2022: `https://www.mas.gov.sg/regulation/guidelines/guidelines-on-provision-of-digital-advisory-services`.

Index

Subscribe to our online digital library for full access to over 7,000 books and videos, as well as industry leading tools to help you plan your personal development and advance your career. For more information, please visit our website.

Why subscribe?

- Spend less time learning and more time coding with practical eBooks and Videos from over 4,000 industry professionals

- Improve your learning with Skill Plans built especially for you

- Get a free eBook or video every month

- Fully searchable for easy access to vital information

- Copy and paste, print, and bookmark content

Did you know that Packt offers eBook versions of every book published, with PDF and ePub files available? You can upgrade to the eBook version at packtpub.com and as a print book customer, you are entitled to a discount on the eBook copy. Get in touch with us at customercare@packtpub.com for more details.

At www.packtpub.com, you can also read a collection of free technical articles, sign up for a range of free newsletters, and receive exclusive discounts and offers on Packt books and eBooks.

Other Books You May Enjoy

If you enjoyed this book, you may be interested in these other books by Packt:

Python for Finance Cookbook - Second Edition

Eryk Lewinson

ISBN: 978-1-80324-319-1

- Preprocess, analyze, and visualize financial data
- Explore time series modeling with statistical (exponential smoothing, ARIMA) and machine learning models
- Uncover advanced time series forecasting algorithms such as Meta's Prophet
- Use Monte Carlo simulations for derivatives valuation and risk assessment
- Explore volatility modeling using univariate and multivariate GARCH models
- Investigate various approaches to asset allocation
- Learn how to approach ML-projects using an example of default prediction
- Explore modern deep learning models such as Google's TabNet, Amazon's DeepAR and NeuralProphet

Developing High-Frequency Trading Systems

Sebastien Donadio, Sourav Ghosh, Romain Rossier

ISBN: 978-1-80324-281-1

- Understand the architecture of high-frequency trading systems
- Boost system performance to achieve the lowest possible latency
- Leverage the power of Python programming, C++, and Java to build your trading systems
- Bypass your kernel and optimize your operating system
- Use static analysis to improve code development
- Use C++ templates and Java multithreading for ultra-low latency
- Apply your knowledge to cryptocurrency trading

Packt is searching for authors like you

If you're interested in becoming an author for Packt, please visit `authors.packtpub.com` and apply today. We have worked with thousands of developers and tech professionals, just like you, to help them share their insight with the global tech community. You can make a general application, apply for a specific hot topic that we are recruiting an author for, or submit your own idea.

Share Your Thoughts

Now you've finished *Robo-Advisor with Python*, we'd love to hear your thoughts! Scan the QR code below to go straight to the Amazon review page for this book and share your feedback or leave a review on the site that you purchased it from.

https://packt.link/r/1-801-81969-6

Your review is important to us and the tech community and will help us make sure we're delivering excellent quality content.

Download a free PDF copy of this book

Thanks for purchasing this book!

Do you like to read on the go but are unable to carry your print books everywhere? Is your eBook purchase not compatible with the device of your choice?

Don't worry, now with every Packt book you get a DRM-free PDF version of that book at no cost.

Read anywhere, any place, on any device. Search, copy, and paste code from your favorite technical books directly into your application.

The perks don't stop there, you can get exclusive access to discounts, newsletters, and great free content in your inbox daily

Follow these simple steps to get the benefits:

1. Scan the QR code or visit the link below

https://packt.link/free-ebook/978-1-80181-969-5

2. Submit your proof of purchase
3. That's it! We'll send your free PDF and other benefits to your email directly

www.ingramcontent.com/pod-product-compliance
Lightning Source LLC
Chambersburg PA
CBHW060541060326
40690CB00017B/3571